HOW TO HAVE A MEETING WITH GOD, BUDDHA, ALLAH

HOW TO HAVE A MEETING WITH GOD, BUDDHA, ALLAH

After the meeting, I realized all the ways of the world. Any questions? Ask me.

WOO MYUNG

How to Have a Meeting with God, Buddha, Allah
by Woo Myung

Copyright 2021 Woo Myung. All rights reserved. This book or parts thereof may not be reproduced in any form, stored in a retrieval system, or transmitted in any form by any means – electronic, mechanical, photocopy, recording, or otherwise – without prior written permission of the author.

First Edition
First Printing Sep. 2021
Published by Cham Books
1202 Kifer Rd., Sunnyvale CA 94086, U.S.A
Tel: (408) 475-8783

ISBN: 978-1-62593-049-1 (Ebook)
ISBN: 978-1-62593-051-4 (Hardcover)
Library of Congress Control Number: 2021916372

TABLE OF CONTENTS

About the Author	15
Preface	17
Introduction	19

PART 1. THE NEW ERA BEGINS — 21

What Is Truth?	22
How to Have a Meeting with God, Buddha, Allah	24
What Is the Solution for the World to Become One?	26
What Is the Mind?	28
The Human Mind Is the False Mind	29
What Is Sin?	32
What Happens When People Die?	33
Are God, Buddha, Allah Different from Each Other?	35
God, Buddha, Allah Do Not Exist in the World Where People Live	36
Where Is Heaven, the Land of Bliss, and Paradise?	37
I Once Lived in the False World but Now Have Gone to the World of Truth and Know All the Principles of the World	39
What Is Salvation?	41
What is Resurrection?	43
What Is Complete Creation?	44
Only When the Saviors Come as Human Beings Can the World and Humankind Be Saved	46
The Era of Human Completion and the Completion of the Universe	48

Which Place Is the Place of Truth?	49
How to Find the Place of Truth. How to Become Complete and Achieve It All	50
The Existence That Takes People to the Land of Truth Is the Real Truth	51
From the IQ Era to the EQ Era	53
The Masters of the World Are Human Beings	54
From the False World to the True World	55
Only What Exists in One's Mind Exists	56
When God, Buddha, Allah, Which Are Truth, Exist within You, Heaven, the Land of Bliss, Paradise Exist within You, and When You Live in that Land	57
What Work Do the Saviors Do?	58
The Existence of Saviors Can Only Be Found inside the Self	59
A Person Who Has Become True Comes to Know All the Ways of the World	60
When Humans Change Their Minds to the True Mind	61
The New World	64
The Human Mind Is the Universe	67
The Land of Truth	68
What Work Does Truth Do?	69
The Incomplete World	70
Everything Is the Spirit and Soul	74
The Salvation of the World Is Carried out by the Masters of the World Who Are Human Beings	76
The Era of Completion	77
It Must Exist within Your Mind for It to Exist	79
The Era of the Creation of the Holy Spirit and Holy Soul	81
It Is Now Time for Human Completion	83
Is Reincarnation Real or Not?	84
The Method for People Not to Die	86
The Way for a Person to Go to Heaven, the True World	87

Everything That People Believe Exists, Actually Does Not Exist	88
Only That Which Exists inside the Mind That Has Become Truth Exists	89
What Is True Creation? The Existence of Saviors Is Neither within a Name nor in a Religion	90

PART 2. THE ROADMAP TO FINDING TRUTH WITHIN   95

God, Buddha, Allah, *Haneolnim*, and Heaven, the Land of Bliss, Paradise, the Land of *Haneolnim* Are within You	96
What Happens When a Person Dies? How Can a Person Live Eternally?	98
The Reason Why People Could Not Become Complete and True Until Now Is Because the Method Did Not Exist	99
A Person Who Is False Cannot Become Truth Unless He Repents	100
What Is Enlightenment?	101
Omniscience and Omnipotence	102
How Can One Be Absolved of One's Sins, Extinguish One's Karma, and Practice Repentance and Penitence?	104
The Reason and Purpose Why Humans Are Born into This World	105
One Who Has Truth in One's Mind Can Know Both Truth and Falseness	107
What Are Heresies and Cults?	109
Salvation	110
The End of the World	111
The Rapture and the Resurrection	112
The Existence That Can Give Salvation	113
Repentance	114
When Everyone Becomes Complete and True, Religions, Philosophies, Ideologies, Education, Politics, and Economies Will Become One	115
How to See and Know God, Buddha, Allah, *Haneolnim*	116
How to Go to Heaven, the Land of Bliss, Paradise, the Land of Divine Beings	117

The Shape and Form of God, Buddha, Allah, *Haneolnim*	118
To Be Reborn and Resurrected	119
For Humans to Be Born, We Need to Have Parents. Likewise, for People to Be Born as Truth, We Need to Have Parents of Truth	120
The Bible, Buddhist Sutras, *JeungSanDoJeon*, and *Won Buddhist Sutras*	121
Are You Becoming Real in the Place You Are Attending Right Now?	122
When the Time to Become Complete Truth Comes, Where You Can Become Truth Is the Place of Completion	123
The Era of the Way, the Truth, and the Life	124
The Era When Everyone Can Become a Divine Being, Saint, and Buddha	125
One Who Throws Himself Away to Find Truth Will Find Jesus, Buddha, and the Divine Being	126
How to Go from Incompletion to Completion	127
Do We Live Forever with This Body?	128
Union with God	129
The Difference between the People Who Are Possessed and the People Who Spoke of Truth and Prophesied the Coming of Truth	130
Truth	131
Faith	132
Creation	133
A Complete Person Has a Beautiful Face and Will Live Well Because One Just Does What One Has to Do without Delusional Thoughts	134
Complete Person	136
In the Buddhist Sutras	138
The Meaning of "Receiving the Seal"	139

PART 3. PHILOSOPHY FOR A RIGHTEOUS CIVILIZATION — **141**

What Is Philosophy?	142
Who Am I?	143
What Is the False Self?	144

What Is the True Self?	145
How Do You Know If Something Is Real or Fake?	146
Who Do You Think Is the Most Successful Person?	147
How Can We Progress Towards a More Truthful World?	148
After Death, Will Our Lives Be the Same as Our Lives Now?	149
What Would Be the Most Valuable Thing for Humankind?	150
Who Governs This World?	151
What Kind of Place Is Hell, Where Is It, and What Should I Do to Not Go There?	152
How Can You Change Your Life?	153
What One Needs to Do in Life	154
What Is the Reason and Purpose Why People Are Born into This World?	155

PART 4. THE ULTIMATE ASPIRATION OF RELIGION: TRUTH — 157

What Is Religion?	158
What Is the Purpose of Religion?	159
What Is the Origin of Religion?	160
Which Religion Is the Best Religion and Why?	161
Do We Need Religion?	163
Why Are There So Many Religions?	164
There Is Only One God in This World, but Why Are There So Many Different Religions?	165
Why Do People Believe in Religion?	166
What Is the Difference between a Religion and a Cult?	167
What Do All Religions Have in Common?	168
Does Religion Unite Us or Separate Us?	169
Why Are There So Many Denominations in Christianity?	170
Does God Exist?	171
Why Has God Created Us?	172
Is It Possible to Prove the Existence of God? Or Is It Impossible?	173

Where Is God?	174
How Can I Find God?	175
What Does God Mean?	176
How Can I Meet God?	177
How Can I Feel the Existence of God?	178
Why Do I Need to Believe in God?	179

PART 5. ANY QUESTIONS? ASK ME.   181

I. THE MIND   183

What Is the Mind?	184
What Can I Do to Cleanse My Mind? How Can I Cleanse My Mind?	185
How to Eliminate Stress	186
Anxiety Relief: How to Deal with Anxiety	187
How to Eliminate Worries	188
How to Be Free from Thoughts: How to Stop Obsessive Thoughts	189
Inner Peace	190
How to Control and Master Your Emotions	191
How to Overcome Guilt and Regret	192
How Not to Be Angry	193
What Does It Mean to Have Complete Freedom Through Awakening?	194
How to Be Happy and Positive All the Time	195
Gratitude	196
The Power of Mind	197
What Is Depression and How to Get Rid of It?	198
How to Be Courageous and Bold	199
How to Deal with Loneliness	200
How to Meditate Properly: True Meditation Method	201
How to Let Go	202
What Is the Purpose of Life?	203
Wisdom: How to Be Wise	204

II. PERSONAL DEVELOPMENT 205

Be in the Moment. How to Live in the Moment	206
How to Break Bad Habits	207
How to Focus and Improve Concentration	208
Positive Thinking: How to Be Positive	209
As Computers Are Enhanced with Artificial Intelligence, People Should Be Enhanced with True Wisdom	210
Be Grateful: the Secret to Happiness	211
How to Live Well	212
Self-Development Tips	213
How to Become Smart and Wise	214
How to Stay Motivated and Not Give Up	215
How to Have Confidence	216
How to Not Be Bored	217
Meditation for Improving Concentration	218
Overcoming Procrastination: How to Stop Being Lazy	219
Productivity Hack: How to be Productive	220
Real Self-Discipline: How to Build Self-Discipline and Make It Possible	221
Know Your Real Value	222
The Way to Improve Your Life	223
How to Love Yourself	224

III. HEALTH & LONGEVITY 225

Longevity Secrets: How to Live Longer	226
Deep Sleep Secret: How to Sleep Well	227
How to Naturally Boost Your Immune System	228
Mental Health Tips: How to Improve Mental Health	229
How to Heal Your Entire Body and Mind	230
The Best Meditation	231
Laughter Is the Best Medicine	232
How to Keep Your Brain Healthy	233

How to Lose Weight	234
How to Quit Smoking, Drugs, and Alcohol	235
How to Naturally Look Younger than Your Age	236
The Way to Heal Yourself	237

IV. RELATIONSHIPS 239

How to Communicate Effectively with People	240
How to Make People Like You	241
How to Get Along Better with People	242
How to Treat Others	243
How to Be Attractive to Everyone	244
What Is Love? True Meaning of Love	245
Racial Prejudice and Discrimination	246
How to Make Friends	247
How to Be in Harmony and Get Along with Others	248
How to Be a Good Parent	249

V. FINANCE & SUCCESS 251

Just as a Computer Needs to Have AI, People Need to Have the AI-Like True Wisdom: A New and Complete Leadership and Followership	252
How to Succeed	256
The Way to Achieve Your Goal	257
Creative Thinking: How to Be Creative	258
The Power of Persuasion: How to Persuade People	259
How to Become Rich	260
Getting a Good Job	261
How to Survive	262
How to Save Money: Key Mindset	263
How to Find Your True Talent and to Be Successful	264
How to Organize or Systematize Your Life	265
How to Be a Fast Learner	266

How to Live a Good Life	267
How to Change Your Life for the Better: Life Advice	268

VI. SPIRITUALITY & BELIEF 269

How to Reach Enlightenment	270
Truth	271
What are the Spirit and Soul?	272
Heaven (The Real Heaven)	273
The Method to See and Know God	274
What Is the Meaning of Life?	275
What Happens When You Die and How Not to Die?	276
Clear Mind: How to Cleanse Your Mind with Meditation	277
How to Find Your True Self	278
Peace of Mind	279
Acts of Kindness	280
How to Bring Religions Together	281
The Most Important Thing in the World	282
The Reason Why People Cannot See the Creators that are Truth	283
What Is Resurrection?	284
What Is the Rapture?	285
Why Do We Live?	286
Change Your Life	287
How to See and Know God	288
How to Understand the Bible Well	289
How to See Heaven and Go There	290

ABOUT THE AUTHOR

Woo Myung became a #1 Amazon bestselling author in 2012 with his book *Stop Living in This Land, Go to the Everlasting World of Happiness, Live There Forever*. He has now written another #1 Amazon bestseller *How to Have a Meeting with God, Buddha, Allah* that is also a #1 Wall Street Journal, #1 Barnes & Noble, and USA Today bestseller.

Meditation innovator, lecturer, and bestselling author of many books about Truth, Woo Myung attained enlightenment after deep introspection about life and existence. After becoming Truth, he dedicated his life to teaching others to become Truth.

Stop Living in This Land, Go to the Everlasting World of Happiness, Live There Forever also received IPPY Awards, Living Now Book Awards, International Book Awards, and three gold medals from the eLit Book Awards. *Where You Become True Is the Place of Truth*, the winner of the Montaigne Medal presented by the Eric Hoffer Award, also received the National Indie Excellence Award.

Further works by the author include *The Book of Wisdom*, *The Way to Become a Person in Heaven While Living*, *World Beyond World*, *The Living Eternal World*, *Heaven's Formula for Saving the World*, and his poetry collection *of Mind*, *Nature's Flow*, and *The Enlightened World*, which have all been published in English. His works are also available in Chinese, French, Hungarian, Italian, Japanese, Korean, Portuguese, Spanish, and Swedish.

PREFACE

The world is in a boisterous state of chaos due to COVID-19 and as everyone now lives with limited freedom, many people are frustrated.

Many people have died and suffered due to COVID-19, and this has caused people to rethink their lives. Therefore, this book, which contains the alternative, is being released into the world.

Something in this world is changing.

The ultimate goal that every human being especially hopes to achieve is to not die and live forever. The purpose of religions is the same; the purpose of Christianity is to go to and live in Heaven, which is the Kingdom of God that is Truth; the purpose of Buddhism is to go to and live in the Land of Bliss, which is the Land of Buddha that is Truth; and the purpose of Islam is to go to and live in Paradise, which is the land of Allah that is Truth. The meaning of these words is that the ultimate purpose of religion is to go to the Land of Truth and live there forever. When one eliminates the karma, habits, and body, which are one's sins, then Truth exists within oneself, and the Land of Truth exists within oneself. Now is the era when this can be achieved.

In Christianity, they call Truth God, in Buddhism they call it Buddha, and in Islam, they call it Allah. Each religion has given different names to Truth, but when the existence of Truth exists in people's minds and they are born in the Land of Truth, then religions and the world can become one. While living, when everyone in this world goes to and lives in the Land of Truth and lives in the world of oneness, then everything can be achieved.

When you are born in the Land of Truth after meeting God, Buddha, Allah, you will know all the ways of the world. You will not have any unresolved questions or doubts, suffering, burden, or stress.

Every question to which people are seeking answers will be resolved.

I hope that all people will go to the Land of Truth that is within them, thereby becoming complete, knowing everything, and eternally never dying while living.

INTRODUCTION

There is no one who knows the principles behind how people are born into this world, how they live, and then die. Humans came from the Original Foundation before they were born into this world. People live inside their own mind worlds that overlap the world, so nothing remains when they die; this is how it is for humans. However, if one has Truth inside his mind and is born in the true world, he can live forever. Whether one lives or dies is determined by what he has in his mind.

Due to COVID-19, many people are dying, and countless people have been infected. It seems that people are wondering and pondering, "What happens when I die?" because many people are living in agony. People do not know anything. Throughout their lives, they took pictures of the things of this world, and have been living inside their own mind worlds. With what they have learned, read in books, and experienced, people live thinking that they know.

However, if you have the mind of the world and are born again from the world, you can know all the ways of the world. Only when you have gone to the universe emptiness, which is the world, can you meet God, Buddha, Allah, which are Truth. Then, when you are born in the Land of Truth, you can live forever. This is because Truth and the Land of Truth exist inside the mind of a person who has become Truth.

The Land of Truth, which is Heaven, the Land of Bliss, Paradise, is not a place you go to after you die. At this very moment, while living, you should be born in the Land of Truth that is within you in order to live in that land. When you live in the Land of Truth, you can know it all, and there is nothing you do not know. You will have no suffering, burden, stress, unresolved questions, or doubts.

The ultimate purpose of human life is to live forever, but no one was able to achieve this. People think they will go to the Land of Truth after death. However, since they are living inside their own mind worlds, which are nonexistent illusions, they end up dying when they die.

While you are alive, eliminate your karma, habits, and body, which are your sins, go to Truth, and be reborn in the Land of Truth. Then you live there forever, whether you are dead or alive.

When you live in the Land of Truth, it is human completion, and the completion of the universe. It is time for the complete world, which has only been dreamt about, to come true for anyone and everyone. Instead of being a person who dies and disappears in vain, I hope that you will learn the method of how not to die while you are alive, be born as Truth, and not die.

PART 1

THE NEW ERA BEGINS

Now it is time to transcend what we currently know by finding Truth within and achieving True Wisdom. With True Wisdom, we can gain core insight into the fundamental principles of the world and accomplish all that humankind has been searching for.

WHAT IS TRUTH?

We learned at school that Truth is an eternal and unchanging existence. I tell people that Truth is not only eternal and unchanging, but it is also a living existence. We learned as truth the fact that the sun rises in the east and sets in the west. However, it is not Truth because both the sun and the earth will eventually disappear. Only the existence that has neither beginning nor end and only the existence that never changes is Truth. People cannot see this existence and cannot find this existence, even if they try for eternity, because people live inside their own mind worlds—they cannot see nor find what belongs to the real world.

In Christianity, the existence of the Holy Spirit and the Holy Father that is God is Truth. In Buddhism, they call the existence of Truth Buddha—*Dharmakaya* and *Sambhogakaya*. In Islam, they call this existence of Truth Allah. In the ideology of a Korean folk religion, they call it *Haneolnim* that is *Jung* (Spirit) and *Shin* (Soul). The leaders of those religions say that no one has ever seen this existence.

God, Buddha, Allah, which are Truth, are the emptiness of this universe itself. The Spirit and Soul exist in this emptiness. The emptiness of this universe is the existence of the Spirit, and the Soul exists as the one God in that emptiness. This existence is omnipresent in the universe and is the existence that is always alive. This existence created all creations in this world. Buddhism says that things came forth from the earth, water, fire, and wind. And according to a Korean folk religion, *Haneolnim* and everything emerged through the harmony of the sky and the earth. These sayings all mean the same thing, although they are expressed differently. All the creations in this world come from the emptiness of the universe and return there. People can see and know this existence when they have it within their minds.

But because people live inside their mind worlds, which overlap the world, people can neither see nor know this existence because the world is not within their minds. If one's karma, habits, and body did not exist, there would be nothing in this world. Without people, there would not be any other creations in this world either, and there would be nothing. One can see the Spirit and Soul of the universe, which are the existence of Truth, when one's self does not exist and when only the universe emptiness remains. You can only see and know this entity when it exists within you. Then when your mind becomes the Spirit and Soul of the universe, the masters of the world will create you anew from there. Following this, the new Heaven, the new earth, and this world are born again as the never-dying Truth inside your mind that has become Truth.

When this world is born from the mind of a person who has been reborn, it is Truth. As the human mind world is false, a person can neither see nor know this existence, Truth. When you discard this falseness, the mind becomes real, and when you are reborn from that mind, you can know that the entire true world exists within you.

HOW TO HAVE A MEETING WITH GOD, BUDDHA, ALLAH

The existence of Truth is referred to as God in Christianity, Buddha in Buddhism, and Allah in Islam. No one has ever seen this existence, and there is no one that knows this existence either. The way to have a meeting with this existence is when there is no self who is false. Then, it is possible.

When one eliminates the karma, habits, and body, which are one's sins and falseness, and when everything of this entire world does not exist, one can see the Spirit and Soul of the universe. One can see the *Dharmakaya* and *Sambhogakaya*. Only the universe itself remains when the false karma, habits, and body in one's mind do not exist. Then God, Buddha, Allah, which are the existence of Truth, exist within oneself. One can see and know this existence when one has it within. Just as you cannot know something if you do not have it within you, you can only know this existence when you have it within yourself.

The Bible tells us that God is within us and that we should not believe God exists in a certain place over here or over there. In the Buddhist sutras, it also says your mind is Buddha, and the Qur'an also says that Allah is within your mind.

If one is to have a meeting with God, Buddha, Allah, one needs to discard the karma, habits, and body, which are one's sins. Then one can meet God, Buddha, Allah in one's mind that is clean. When one's mind becomes Truth that is within, the existences, who are human beings, that are the creators and the masters of this world will create anew in that land. Then the world that is reborn as Truth inside one's mind is Heaven, the Land of Bliss, Paradise. Truth, which is God, Buddha, Allah, is within your mind. Heaven, the Land of Bliss, Paradise, which is the world that is reborn in that Land of Truth, is also within your mind. Only the one who is born in this land, while living, can be born in this land and live. When one's mind becomes the Spirit and Soul of the universe while living, and this world is created again in this land, then this place, right here, is Heaven.

When one is reborn as Truth inside oneself, this is being raptured, this is the resurrection, this is having received the seal, this is salvation, this is the eternally living Heaven, and this is where life and death are actually one. Human completion, the completion of the world, and the completion of the universe have already come to pass.

The Spirit and Soul of the universe, which are the masters of this world, carried out material creation. But creation of the Holy Spirit and Holy Soul takes place only when this existence comes as human beings. It is completion because everything will be brought to life and lives within a person's mind—this is how this universe can be created anew and becomes complete. The way to have a meeting with Truth and go to the Land of Truth is to repent for one's sins, which means to discard the karma, habits, and body.

WHAT IS THE SOLUTION FOR THE WORLD TO BECOME ONE?

After being born into the world, people have constantly been fighting as they live their lives. Ever since they were young, they have been fighters who had to defeat others. They lived their entire lives agonizing and battling, trying not to fall behind in competition. When living in this world, people are fighters who are in constant combat, who do not want to be defeated. This is why, whether in our lives at home or in our social lives, everyone is a fighter who is battling. No one in this world is an easy pushover. Consequently, even to this day, countries are fighting each other, and religious wars never cease to exist.

Although everyone believes in God, Buddha, Allah, which are Truth, no one has become one with that existence. Instead, people are only crying out that name from within the false worlds where humans live, places where there is no Truth. They are just praying and calling out that name from within places where there is no existence of Truth that is God, Buddha, Allah.

It is written in the Bible that God, which is Truth, exists within people's minds. It also says in the Buddhist sutras that Buddha and Allah in the Qur'an are within one's mind. Instead of seeking Truth in the name, people of this world should actually become God, Buddha, Allah (Truth) within their minds. The world will then become one. Unless one seeks Truth from within himself, he cannot find it. One cannot find it because he will look for it within the nonexistent human conceptions, habits, and customs where there is no Truth.

In the era of incompletion before these current times, the masters of the world, who are the Way, the Truth, and the Life, did not exist. Therefore, there was no Truth or method to repent that could allow people to go to the Land of Truth.

A person who is born and living in the false world cannot achieve Truth unless there are the masters of the world who can give life. The way for this world to become one is for the falseness to become Truth. Even if religions join together, they cannot become one. There will be fierce battles due to the countless denominations. However, the world will become one when people are made to have Truth within their minds. Then there will be no distinctions between "your country" and "my country," and "your religion" and "my religion."

WHAT IS THE MIND?

Absolutely nothing but the *Jung* (Spirit) and *Shin* (Soul) exists in the true mind. This *Jung* and *Shin* are the Spirit and Soul that exist in the universe emptiness. This *Jung* and *Shin* are Truth. Each religion calls Truth a different name—God in Christianity, Buddha in Buddhism, and Allah in Islam. However, they are all one. This is the true mind of humans. When one throws away his false karma, habits, and body, the real Truth exists within his mind.

THE HUMAN MIND IS THE FALSE MIND

In the human mind, there are the life lived (karma), the habits (inherited from one's ancestors), and the body. These make up the human mind. People live inside their own mind worlds, which overlap the world. They are not the true world, but worlds of illusions that their minds have made. That is why people live in false worlds, do false things and when they die, they just end up completely dying. This is why they are incomplete. A person's mind is one's own fixed conceptions, habits, and customs that only he himself possesses.

There are no two single people in the world who have the same minds. The human mind only exists for the person who possesses it. It is an illusion made up of pictures of the things in the world, and this is why it does not exist. Just as a person cannot change one's dream while in the dream, a person who lives in that mind just lives in that mind. This mind is false and, therefore, does not exist.

The true mind does not exist, yet it exists. The false mind, which is the human mind, exists, yet it does not exist.

The true mind is a nonmaterial, real existence and it is Truth.

The false mind is an illusion made by the human mind.

Once you completely eliminate yourself who is living in the false world with the false mind, only the true mind remains. When the world and yourself are born again from the true mind, that land is the land of the eternal, living Heaven. It is the land where the creators have created this world again. This land is within the human mind.

The false self does not exist, and everything is alive.
It is the era to transition from
material creation to creation of the Holy Spirit and Holy Soul.
One's mind becomes Truth and is born again from Truth.
This world then becomes Truth and exists within one's mind.
One's past material self has disappeared,
and only the true mind remains.
And as one has been born again from Truth,
this entire world has been saved.
The masters of the world have come as human beings
and have saved everything.
The masters' words are life.
Until now, there has been only Spirit and Soul in this world.
But now, the masters have created the material in that world
as the *Jung* (Spirit) and *Shin* (Soul).
The universe is born again, and everything is alive.
The creators alone have created the new Heaven and new earth.
The creators have brought forth new birth
within the human mind.
The way for one to go to Heaven,
the way for one to become Truth,
the way for one to go to the Land of Divine Beings,
and the way for one to go to
the Kingdom of God, Buddha, Allah are all the same.
The way is for one's false karma, habits, and body
to completely disappear.
Then, the true mind remains.
When the world and oneself are born again from the true mind,
this land is Heaven, the Land of Bliss, and Paradise.
One can live eternally in this land, right here.
When an incomplete person dies,

he ends up dying because he is incomplete.
A complete person is always alive without life or death.
One is always alive inside one's mind.
One is alive because
he is the energy and light of the universe itself.
Even though one exists,
he does not have the mind that he exists; he simply just exists.
All the minds do not exist.
It is freedom and liberation whether the self exists or not.
It is freedom and liberation because one now lives free
from all past human conceptions, customs, and habits.
One is the energy and light of the universe itself, which is Truth.
One is the eternally living, never-dying God.

WHAT IS SIN?

Human sin is that people live inside their own self-centered minds instead of living in the universe mind, which is the world. This is why humans are sinners. The sin is that they do not live in Truth, which is the *Jung* (Spirit) and *Shin* (Soul) of the universe, but live inside their own minds, which are not the world.

The human mind is the karma, habits, and body. This is one's mind. The karma, which is the life lived, the habits that one inherited from ancestors, and the body are the sin. People are not real Truth, but false because they live inside their minds, which are the picture worlds that overlap the world. Also, they live copying the things of the world that is Truth. When one eliminates this falseness and becomes real, one's mind is Truth.

The people who are the masters of the world can make this world be born again as the real world inside the mind of a person who has become real. The Spirit and Soul of the universe itself remain when all of one's karma, habits, and body completely die. When this Spirit and Soul, which are Truth, become one's mind, the nonexistent world is created from there and one becomes complete.

WHAT HAPPENS WHEN PEOPLE DIE?

Each religion and many people believe that when a person dies, there is a world after death. In the era of incompletion, because people did not have wisdom, when people were told it was so, they accepted and believed it to be true. And those beliefs have continued until now. However, in the era of completion, one can know the fact of the matter, and know that what one was told was not correct.

Let us suppose there is a dead person here. This person cannot think and cannot cry out in pain even if pierced with a knife. And if this person were burned in a fire, there would be nothing remaining. It is the way of the world that all material things in this world come to this world once and then disappear.

The Spirit and Soul of the universe carried out the material creation of this world. When the masters of the world, who are the saviors, come as human beings and create this world and the people anew as the Spirit and Soul, which is Truth, then they will have the Spirit and Soul. If the material things in this world and people already had the Spirit and Soul, the saviors would not need to come to the world.

The transition from the era of material creation to the era of creation of the Holy Spirit and Holy Soul ushers in the era of human completion and the completion of the universe; all that have been created through the creation of the Holy Spirit and Holy Soul are Truth and eternally living, immortal entities.

Creation of the Holy Spirit and Holy Soul is the rapture, salvation, the resurrection, and having received the seal. When a person has been reborn within one's mind, which is the Land of Truth, he is born in Heaven and lives there. This world is then a complete world, and this universe becomes complete because it will live forever without dying. Only when a person, while alive, discards the karma, habits, and body that are one's sins, can one be born again and live in the Land of Truth.

Now is the time when completion is being achieved. It is people's duty as a member of humankind to repent, go to the true world, and live forever. It is also the reason and purpose for being born in and living in this world.

ARE GOD, BUDDHA, ALLAH DIFFERENT FROM EACH OTHER?

There are countless religions and religious denominations throughout the world, and they each think that theirs is the correct one. Although it cannot be seen with the eyes, there are religious wars taking place; so the world cannot be united.

The ultimate source and origin of this world are the creators who are the masters of the Original Foundation. They are the *Jung* (Spirit) and *Shin* (Soul) of the emptiness of the universe that is Truth. They are the Spirit and Soul and the *Dharmakaya* and *Sambhogakaya*. The masters are this existence. This existence is an omniscient and omnipotent entity, the creators, and the entity of Truth, which existed since the beginning and will exist for eternity. This existence, which is Truth, is referred to as God in Christianity, Buddha in Buddhism, and Allah in Islam. Truth has always existed and is an entity that exists forever. There is no other existence that is more supreme and holier than this omniscient, omnipresent, living existence. In each religion's scripture—the Bible, the Buddhist sutras, the Qur'an—it says that the existence of God, Buddha, Allah exists within the mind. There is no one in this world who has seen this existence that is Truth. A person cannot see this existence because one is blinded by the karma, habits, and body, which are his sins. Once one discards and eliminates the karma, habits, and body of oneself who is the sinner, he can see and know this existence.

GOD, BUDDHA, ALLAH DO NOT EXIST IN THE WORLD WHERE PEOPLE LIVE

A person does not have the existence of Truth that is God, Buddha, Allah because he is living inside his mind world, which overlaps the world, and there is no real Truth in that mind world. God, Buddha, Allah are Truth. Truth exists within one's mind that has become Truth. A person living in the false human mind world that is not real can have God, Buddha, Allah, which are Truth, within his mind when he discards and eliminates the human mind.

WHERE IS HEAVEN, THE LAND OF BLISS, AND PARADISE?

There are many people who claim that they went to Heaven, the Land of Bliss, or Paradise after they died. Some patients with heart disease are often not able to wake up even after CPR. But they would wake up later and allege that they had gone to Heaven, the Land of Bliss, or Paradise during that time. However, those people had not died but had seen the illusory world of Heaven, the Land of Bliss, or Paradise that they created within their minds. This is not the world of Truth, and as it does not exist, it disappears when it is eliminated.

Truth that is Heaven, the Land of Bliss, and Paradise that is God's World, Buddha's World, Allah's World is the world that exists within one's mind that has become Truth. The masters of the world must make this world be born again for this universe and the self to be born again as Truth and be saved.

The era of material creation has ended. In this Land of Truth that has been created as the Holy Spirit and Holy Soul, this land right here, all will live eternally with the body that has become Truth. Only the one who is born in this land while living will live without life or death.

One will live eternally within his mind. No matter how much one tries to eliminate this land, it is the Land of Truth, which cannot be eliminated.

The one who does not have Truth or the Land of Truth within himself will end up dying. One can only live when he is born in and always living in Heaven, the Land of Bliss, and Paradise while living.

In Buddhist temples, people pray, bow, and hold rituals for a better afterlife. In the Catholic Church, they say no one will live unless one is born of water and the Holy Spirit. A person is immersed in water, and when he comes out, they ask the person, "Do you believe in Jesus Christ?" If the person answers, "I believe," it is said that this person has been born as the Holy Spirit. Depending upon each denomination, some submerge a person in water, while others just sprinkle some water on the head. When the person says, "I believe in Jesus Christ," it is believed that this is how the person is born as the Holy Spirit. If one could be born as the Holy Spirit in this manner, there would be no need for the saviors to come to this world.

The universe Spirit and Soul are the creators of all the material forms in this world. The Original Foundation, which is the master of this world, is where all the material forms that are born in this world come from and return to. Once these forms return to the Original Foundation, they disappear. It is a matter of living or dying. There is no Spirit or Soul within people. So, once the material form appears and then disappears, it simply disappears.

When Truth, who are the saviors, come to this world, they will have people repent and absolve them of their sins. Only when the saviors create this world and the people in that land will the Spirit and Soul exist. Until now, there was no completion, which is salvation, because it was the material era. Starting now is the era of the creation of the Holy Spirit and Holy Soul.

A person can have Truth within his mind, and he can have Heaven and Paradise, the Land of Truth, only when it is created. One who has this within his mind is the one who is living, and he who does not have it is the one who is dead. You can only live when you have God, Buddha, Allah, which are Truth, within you. You can only live when you have that land within you.

I ONCE LIVED IN THE FALSE WORLD BUT NOW HAVE GONE TO THE WORLD OF TRUTH AND KNOW ALL THE PRINCIPLES OF THE WORLD

Just as computers have artificial intelligence (AI), humans can now have a similar intelligence, which is True Wisdom. People living in this world live thinking that they are living in the world. However, people do not live in the world, but rather, they live inside of their own mind worlds, which overlap the world. This is why humans are incomplete. The mind world is different for each person. Each person thinks that only what he knows is correct as there is no Truth within him.

In one's religious or social life, a person says something is right if it suits his mind and is incorrect if it does not fit his mind. This comes from the self-centered mind that a person came to have from the life that he lived. When one discards this, becomes the mind of the world, which is Truth, and is reborn from the true world, he can know all the ways of the world.

When one was false, he did not know anything and had unresolved questions and doubts; one lived with suffering and burdens. Now that one is born and living in the Land of Truth, there are no unresolved questions or doubts, and he has no more suffering or burdens.

Falseness knows neither falseness nor Truth, but Truth knows both falseness and Truth. Falseness, which is dead, knows nothing. But Truth knows all the ways of the world. Human AI is the wisdom of Truth because one has become Truth. With this Human AI, I am resolving the unanswered questions and doubts of many people from all over the world. I am also answering questions about religion, ideology, and philosophy that come in through YouTube and Facebook—solving all questions, uncertainties, and doubts that people have come to have while living in this world with their suffering, stress, and burdens.

WHAT IS SALVATION?

Salvation is when the dead world and dead people are brought to life. The reason why the world is not alive is because people are incomplete.

People are incomplete because they do not live in the world, but rather live inside their mind worlds that overlap the world. This world is a film of one's life lived etched in one's mind, which does not actually exist. And a person lives thinking that he knows things based on what he has experienced. Therefore, since a person lives confined to his own mind world, he does false deeds in the false world and then simply ends up dying.

People are dead because they live inside their own minds, which are the false worlds. People think that all the creations in this world exist because they themselves exist. However, those creations do not exist because it is simply from within their false worlds that people think that those creations exist. When people who are false do not exist in the false world, neither the creations of this world nor the emptiness exist.

This world is not alive just because the false human mind thinks it exists. And, in fact, all the things that exist in the world, regardless of whether they are existent or nonexistent, do not actually exist.

Salvation is to save all of this. In order to save all, people, who are false, need to disappear from this world to let only the emptiness of the universe—the Origin, the Spirit and the Soul—remain. Then when people are born again from the mind of the Spirit and Soul by the words of the masters of Truth, it is salvation.

Salvation is to make a nonexistent world be born again in the Land of Truth. This world that is born again within a person's mind is the eternally existing Land of Truth, Heaven, the Land of Bliss, Paradise.

WHAT IS RESURRECTION?

Resurrection is when all the creations of the universe within this world are made to live as Truth in the Land of Truth. The world can only be saved when the masters of the world come as human beings. The masters will make this world be born again within the mind of a person who is Truth. The words of the masters are life; when everything is told to be born again, all are born again and live. The parents of Truth can give birth to them.

The infinite Spirit and Soul of this universe has existed since the beginning, existed forever before, and will exist forever after. Seen from the perspective of this universe, even though the celestial bodies of the stars, sun, earth, and moon exist, they do not exist; they are the nonexistent Spirit and Soul. Although all things and people of the earth exist, they are simply the Spirit and Soul. Regardless of whether all things of this world exist, or not, they are the nonexistent Spirit and Soul. They are the Spirit and Soul because they have not been born as individual entities from the Original Foundation. Since all things are within the universe, they are the universe itself. This universe exists when it exists inside a person's mind. When the individual entity is told to be born again, it will be reborn within the mind of a person who has become Truth; and it will live. This world does not exist unless one exists. The master that saves this world must be the master of the Land of Truth. The masters' words are Truth, and these words are life. So when the masters tell something to be born in the Land of Truth, it is born. This is the true resurrection.

WHAT IS COMPLETE CREATION?

Creation is making something that does not exist, exist. The Spirit and Soul, which are the masters of the emptiness, created all the material forms of this world. Everything in this world comes from that emptiness and returns there. The material forms of this world are not complete, so they exist and then disappear. For the complete and perfect creation of this world, it must be born again from inside the mind of a person who has become Truth. Only this land is an eternally living land, which is without death. This land is Heaven, the Land of Bliss and Paradise.

Humans, who are living inside their false mind worlds instead of living in this world, are illusory and false. When this false person has been absolved of one's sins, and that mind becomes real, the creators will make this person be born again in that land. Then this world and the person who has been born again inside one's mind that has become Truth can become complete and live forever. This is the completion of the universe and the completion of humankind. It is completion because this whole world will live forever.

The people who are the masters of Truth can carry out real creation from within the mind of a person who has become Truth. This new Heaven and new earth can be created when the entire universe is reborn as life from the mind of a person who has become Truth. In this way, there is no death. It is the completion of the universe and the completion of all creations and humankind.

It is claimed that this world has been created, but this is only from the perspective of the human mind. The world has not been created and does not exist. Only the masters of the world can save all there is in the world by making everything be born again. Truth is within you. God, Buddha, Allah are within you. The land that is created again inside one's mind is Heaven, the Land of Bliss, Paradise. This is how this universe becomes complete. This is the complete creation. This is the rapture because this world and people are born in Heaven, which is Truth. This is the resurrection, being marked with the seal, salvation, and the everlasting, living Heaven.

ONLY WHEN THE SAVIORS COME AS HUMAN BEINGS CAN THE WORLD AND HUMANKIND BE SAVED

In the Bible, it is said that we should not believe that God exists in a certain place over here or over there. It says that God exists within your mind. A pastor once said that there is no one who knows God or has seen God, although there are countless churches and Christians in this world.

This existence, God, is the entity of Truth. It is the Spirit and Soul of the universe that is the master of the world. To find this existence, one needs to eliminate the karma, habits, and body, which are one's mind. Then, only the universe remains, and the Spirit and Soul of the universe exist in one's mind. This is when one can see and know God, which is Truth.

This existence is a nonmaterial, real entity. The Spirit, which is the body of the universe, exists in the middle of nothingness. And the Soul exists there as the one consciousness. When these entities come as human beings, they would be the saviors. And only then can this world be saved.

The *Jung* (Spirit) and *Shin* (Soul) of the universe existed even before the beginning and will continue to exist even after. When the *Jung* and *Shin* of the universe come as human beings, the karma, habits, and body, which are human sins, will be eliminated. People will then become the mind of Truth and be made to be reborn from there—this is salvation.

In Buddhism, it is said that *Maitreya* will come to the world and save humankind. And in a Korean prophecy book, it is said, "It will come. It will come. A person will come from the sky." This means that *Jungdoryung*, who is the master of the righteous

Truth, will come. Islam also tells people that Allah has to be found within the self.

When this existence comes and brings salvation, where are people to be saved? It will be in the land where all the false human mind has been discarded and where one's mind has become the mind of Truth. This world and one's self who has repented will be saved in this land.

The saviors cannot be found in the world where people are living, no matter how hard they try to find them. This is because rather than living in the world where Truth, which is God, Buddha, Allah, lives, people are living inside their own illusionary mind worlds. This is why the saviors cannot be found from there, no matter how hard people search for it. When one's false mind does not exist, the mind, which is Truth itself, is the very existence that each religion names. This existence is the masters of the world who will create again in the Land of Truth.

Only this existence can have people repent when it comes as human beings. And only when it comes as human beings is it possible to take people to Heaven that is within them and create the world of Truth again from there. The saviors, who are the masters of Truth, can also only be found within oneself.

People who are living in the human world will never find this existence even if they search for eternity. Only when a person repents and is absolved of one's sins can one see and know God, Buddha, Allah, the saviors who are Truth.

THE ERA OF HUMAN COMPLETION AND THE COMPLETION OF THE UNIVERSE

What needs to happen for humankind and the universe to become complete?

The human mind is the mind of falseness, which has copied the things of this world. It is the habits that one has received from one's ancestors and the karma, which is the life lived. This body is also a sin because it lives in the false world. When the karma, habits, and body are discarded, and there is no existence of the self, the Spirit and Soul of the universe remain. When the masters of Truth then create in this land that is Truth, this land is Heaven, the Land of Bliss, Paradise, which is the Land of Truth.

All the material things of this world can only live up to their life spans and then just disappear. However, the creation of Truth, where everything is eternal and does not disappear, is ultimately fulfilled in the mind world of humans. This is why humans are the masters, and it is the completion of this universe, the completion of humankind, and the completion of all creations in the universe.

The new Heaven, new earth, and new world where people become complete are not achieved in the world where people live. The true world is created from the mind of a person who has repented, or in other words, has been absolved of one's sins.

WHICH PLACE IS THE PLACE OF TRUTH?

While living in this world, there are cases where people insist that their particular religion is right and are therefore in conflict with each other. Even now, there are countries fighting over religion. Which place in this world has the true religion?

Religions have given the existence of Truth a name: in Christianity, they call it God; in Buddhism, they call it Buddha; in Islam, they call it Allah. Although the names are all different, without a doubt, they all seek and believe in Truth.

In each religious scripture, it says that God, Buddha, Allah, which are Truth, exist within the mind. It also says that Heaven, the Land of Bliss, Paradise are also within the mind. The place of Truth would be the place where one can become Truth. If one is to become Truth, he should discard the karma, habits, and body, which are one's sins, and have God, Buddha, Allah, which are the entity of Truth, within his mind. One should also have Heaven, the Land of Bliss, Paradise within one's mind. Only the place that does this would be the place of Truth.

In the place that is real, one either has Truth and the Land of Truth within oneself, or one would be in the process of repenting for one's sins to go to that land. The place where they only talk about Truth, instead of actually going to the Land of Truth that exists within the mind, is not the real place. The place where you can find Truth within the mind is the real place. The place where you can find Truth and have it within you is the place of Truth.

HOW TO FIND THE PLACE OF TRUTH. HOW TO BECOME COMPLETE AND ACHIEVE IT ALL

Truth: Christianity calls it God, Buddhism calls it Buddha, and Islam calls it Allah.

Truth is within you, and the Land of Truth is within you.

= God is within you, and the Kingdom of God is within you.

= Buddha is within you, and the Land of Buddha is within you.

= Allah is within you, and the Land of Allah is within you.

Truth and the Land of Truth have to exist within your mind at all times.

One should be born into the Land of Truth.

Only what exists within you exists.

It is the eternally living world.

For this to be realized, one must discard the karma, habits, and body, which are the human mind.

THE EXISTENCE THAT TAKES PEOPLE TO THE LAND OF TRUTH IS THE REAL TRUTH

In Christianity, it says that God is within you, and in Buddhism, it says that Buddha is within you. In Islam, it says Allah is within you. It is also said that the Kingdom of God, Buddha, Allah is within you. Each religion has given different names to Truth—God, Buddha, Allah.

The saviors are the ones who will eliminate the nonexistent world that people have made so that they can go to the true world that is the existent world.

Christianity has said that when Christ returns in the Second Coming, he will bring people to Heaven by cleansing their sins—just like washing clothes with lye. In Buddhism, it says that humankind will be saved and brought to the Land of Bliss. In Islam, it says that people will go to Paradise. Each religion says that Heaven is within you, the Land of Bliss is within you, Paradise is within you.

It is said that when they come, the saviors will have people repent and then take them to the Land of Truth that is within them. In achieving this, whether you call them the Saviors, the Second Coming of Jesus, *Maitreya*, or Truth, the name is irrelevant. Someone who takes you to the Land of Truth would be Truth. What matters is not the name, but the fact that you can be taken to Truth by this person. People constructed different names for this person who takes people to Truth. However, the ability to take people to Truth has nothing to do with names. If you are bound to those names, you will never find this existence. You could wait for eternity, but this existence will never come. Instead, repent and find Truth and the Land of Truth from within your mind.

Truth, which is God, Buddha, Allah, is within you. The Land of Truth that is the land of God, land of Buddha, land of Allah is also within you. If it is not Truth, it is all falseness.

FROM THE IQ ERA TO THE EQ ERA

Until now, in the world of material creation, it was an era when people who had high IQs (Intelligence Quotient) lived a better life. However, now we have entered the era when IQ is not very useful because there are computers that contain a surplus of information. In the U.S., statistics show that those who had better personalities eventually became more successful than those who had good grades while attending school. Now people with high EQs (Emotional Quotient or Emotional Intelligence) can become successful.

The human mind lives knowing only itself because it has a narrow, self-centered mind. However, if one escapes from the false mind that is not real and, instead, has the mind of the living Spirit and Soul of the universe, one will live a life of nature's flow. One will have wisdom, so he will not experience conflicts or blockages with others. One will live well because wisdom will come when he just diligently does his work without thinking. Instead of living in a self-centered way, everyone will live life with a generous mind that lives for others.

To have a high EQ, eliminate the human karma, habits, and body so that only the true mind remains. From that true mind, one lives the life of wisdom so one will not have unresolved questions, doubts, suffering, or burdens, and one will live a liberated, generous life. A person who lives in the EQ era will live a happy life.

THE MASTERS OF THE WORLD ARE HUMAN BEINGS

The masters of this world are the creators, who are the Spirit and Soul of the universe. In the era when the Spirit and Soul of the universe itself was the master, all material things in the world came from there and returned there. These material things are incomplete because they cannot live forever.

If everything in existence and nonexistence in this world and humankind are to be saved, people should eliminate their minds and bodies, which are their sins. Then, people's minds will become the Spirit and Soul of the universe. And when the ones who are the masters of the world create everything anew, then Truth and the Land of Truth exist within people's minds. The world is born again because there are people. So people are the masters.

FROM THE FALSE WORLD TO THE TRUE WORLD

People live in this world thinking that they are born into this world and are living there. However, people are false because they are living inside the mind world, which overlaps the world.

The human mind world is composed of the karma, habits, and body. Once one discards the karma, habits, and body, the universe *Jung* (Spirit) and *Shin* (Soul), which are Truth, exist within his mind.

When the masters of Truth make a person be reborn, this world and one's self are reborn as Truth. Then the false self becomes Truth. This also applies to the worlds that people live in. Before, people were living in the mind worlds that were not real, but now they can be reborn in the true world and live. They can go from false worlds to being born into and living in the true world. What was illusory becomes real, and the false world is reborn as the true world and lives.

ONLY WHAT EXISTS IN ONE'S MIND EXISTS

Inside their false human minds, people believe that they have faith in God, Buddha, Allah, which are Truth. However, there is no real Truth in their minds, so no matter how much they shout and cry out, God, Buddha, Allah do not exist there. And no matter how hard they pray, as it is done in the false worlds, their prayers will not reach the true world.

God, Buddha, Allah, which are Truth, appear when one discards the falseness that is the human mind. When the masters of Truth make everything to be born again from here, then this place, here, is Heaven, the Land of Bliss, Paradise. This land is the Land of Truth, the real world. Truth and the Land of Truth have to exist within your mind for it to exist. If it does not exist there, it does not exist.

WHEN GOD, BUDDHA, ALLAH, WHICH ARE TRUTH, EXIST WITHIN YOU, HEAVEN, THE LAND OF BLISS, PARADISE EXIST WITHIN YOU, AND WHEN YOU LIVE IN THAT LAND:

1. You can know all the ways of the world.
2. You can always live in Heaven and Paradise while living.
3. You can solve all the curiosities, unresolved questions and doubts that people have.
4. You are equipped with Human AI, which is Truth, so there is nothing that you will not know.
5. It allows for the completion of the universe and human completion to be achieved within you.
6. It is the method of going to Truth, and it is also Truth and life
7. It unites the world so that it becomes one.
8. For the people who were living with suffering and burdens, that suffering and those burdens disappear.
9. You are always happy because you live in the eternally living world.

WHAT WORK DO THE SAVIORS DO?

The saviors are the masters who save this world. This world can only be saved when the existence of the Way, the Truth, and the Life comes. In other words, it can only be saved when the masters of the world come.

In the era before now, the masters were the *Jung* (Spirit) and *Shin* (Soul) of the universe. Now is the era when the existence of the *Jung* and *Shin* of the universe must come as human beings to make this world and people become complete—to be reborn as the eternally never disappearing Truth within a person's mind. This is the era when Heaven on earth becomes actuality. Even Heaven and Paradise would be false if they are not Truth.

Salvation is making things that exist in the world become existent and bringing forth life in the Land of Truth. This is the work of the saviors.

The *Jung* and *Shin* in this world have created all creations in this universe. Only when this existence comes as human beings, will all beings, who are not yet born in the real world that is the Land of Truth, be created. This existence will have them all be born again in that land, the place that exists within one's mind. This world itself exists within the mind of a person who has become Truth. Heaven on earth is fulfilled. And the dream of living forever with this body, in this land right here, without life or death can come true.

Until now, there was no such thing as completion. But now is the time when the eternally never-dying world can be achieved inside a person's mind. Only the one who has been completely absolved of his sins can go to this land.

THE EXISTENCE OF SAVIORS CAN ONLY BE FOUND INSIDE THE SELF

The saviors are the masters who save the world. This entire world can be saved only by the masters of this world. It can only be saved when the masters of the world come as human beings.

Although the Spirit and Soul of the universe are the creators of material matter, when this existence comes as human beings, these creators of the Holy Spirit and Holy Soul can make this world become complete.

Creation of the Holy Spirit and Holy Soul can only be achieved when the material creators come as human beings. If one is to know the creators of the Holy Spirit and Holy Soul within oneself, one should first know the material creators. The creators of the Holy Spirit and Holy Soul that save the entire world can then be found when one knows that these people are this existence itself.

These creators are the saviors who make the world and people, who are living in a nonexistent false world, be born in the true world. This is the rapture, the resurrection, salvation, having received the seal, and being born in and living in eternal Heaven. These saviors are the ones who save this world by making it be born in the Land of Truth.

A PERSON WHO HAS BECOME TRUE COMES TO KNOW ALL THE WAYS OF THE WORLD

The reason why people have unresolved questions, doubts, suffering, and burdens is that they live inside their incomplete minds. These mind worlds are illusionary worlds that are not alive. The mind is the habits and body, which one inherited from one's parents, in addition to one's life lived until now. There are no two single people who are of the same mind.

People are incomplete because they live inside their minds, which are illusionary worlds. This is why people do not know anything. One lives thinking that he knows things based on only what he has experienced, but even what he thinks he knows is also false because it comes from falseness. When one eliminates all of one's mind, which is false, becomes Truth, and is born again, then he has no more unresolved questions, doubts, suffering, or burdens.

One does not know anything because he is false. Once one becomes Truth, he can know it all. It is the world where falseness becomes Truth. The truth behind all the tales that were told in the false world until now will be brought to light when the true world comes—now is such a time. A person who has become Truth will know it all.

WHEN HUMANS CHANGE THEIR MINDS TO THE TRUE MIND

Everything becomes one when people's minds become the true mind. The world will become united as one. Religions, philosophies, ideologies, and academics will all become one. Countries will also unite as one. There will be no more conflicts or wars. Instead, there will be only peace.

Each and every person living in this world has a different mind because each mind has different habits and karma, which is one's life lived. With those different minds, people have created their own minds. These minds are incomplete, made up of the pictures one has taken while living in this world.

People live inside their own mind worlds, which overlap the world. People live thinking that they know things based on what they have experienced, but that is all false and not real. People do false deeds in the false world and then disappear because they are false. Since there is no Truth in the human mind, everything that is man-made is false.

If one wants to be real, it is only possible when real Truth is within his mind. Then one can become Truth.

All religions, ideologies, philosophies, and academics in the world are incomplete. One can only become complete when one has the mind of Truth and is born in and lives in the Land of Truth.

Religions are supposed to be about seeking Truth; however, instead of trying to look for Truth and become Truth, each religion has given Truth a different name—God, Buddha, Allah—and they believe in the name. People cry out that name, pray to it, sing praises about it, bow down to it, and build luxurious chapels, yet they do not have God, Buddha, Allah, which are Truth, within them.

It is said that Truth exists within your mind. But people do not have it within their minds. They do not have the Land of Truth either. For Truth to exist, one should eliminate the karma, habits, and body, which is the false human mind. Once eliminated, one can live because he has Truth within him and the Land of Truth within his mind.

No country is complete because all countries, communism, democracies, and socialism were created by people who were incomplete. To unite all the countries in the world and to unite all religions as one, people should discard their countless false minds and change to the true mind; then everyone can become one.

Even when people pretend to be Truth and righteous in appearance, ultimately, there is no Truth within people's countless, continuously changing false minds.

People can become Truth because there is an alternative for them to become the real Truth. When one discards his incomplete karma, habits, and body, which are living inside his mind, his mind will become Truth. One's self and the world will become Truth when born again from this mind, which has now become Truth, and everything can become united as one.

Each country has different ideologies such as democracy, communism, capitalism, etc. Although each country believes that its own system is right, all of them are incomplete.

It is the same for religions. All religions will be right when people's minds become Truth. Everything and everyone will become one. Oneness is not abstract or conceptual. Religious people in each country will lead all people to become Truth. Everyone will become one, and everyone will become a true person. The world will become a country where everyone is united as one. There will be no conflicts, and people will help each other. Everyone will live for others.

In the Bible, it is said that not all those who cry out for the Lord will go to Heaven. It is said that only those who truly, truly believe will go. This means that only the ones who have the Lord, which is Truth, within their minds will go to Heaven.

One who has Truth in his mind is the one who has true faith. Only the one who has eliminated his sins, which are the karma, habits, and body has Truth within. When the false self completely dies, one can be born again as the true self and live in the Land of Truth. This person is one who has achieved it all and is complete. When this world is born again inside one's mind world, this world can live eternally as Truth. This is the world where people are alive, a world without death; there is no life or death.

Following the era of material creation, it is now the era of the creation of the Holy Spirit and Holy Soul. It is said that this body will live forever in this land, right here. This means this land and body in material form that is one with the form of the *Jung* (Spirit) and *Shin* (Soul), will live eternally. Life and death are one.

Now is the era, whilst living, when this world and all creations of the universe can become complete. Only when your self of the past has completely died can you be reborn in the new world and live. Only the one whose false self has completely died can go. Only Truth can live.

THE NEW WORLD

For all existent and nonexistent things of the world to be saved during the era of creation, the creators of Heaven and earth must come as human beings. Only then can everything be saved.

The minds of human beings were made in the image of God that is the world. These words mean that human beings have copied this world and have been living inside of those copies. This makes one a sinner, and because he is living in his own mind, it is a dead, illusory world he is living in. It does not exist because it is a world that only exists inside his mind.

When one eliminates his mind (the karma, habits, and body), which is the sin and not real, only the true mind remains. This true mind is the Spirit and Soul of the universe. This itself is the creator and Truth.

When the self completely dies, the universe remains. The universe itself becomes your mind, and your mind and the universe are one. Then your mind is Truth and Heaven.

When the masters of Truth come to this world as human beings, those existences are the saviors who save the world.

The Spirit and Soul of the universe have begotten and created the material forms. However, the creators, which are the Spirit and Soul of the universe, are the ones who fully complete the world by creating it anew within the human mind.

The world that is born again from the mind that has become Truth is Truth and is eternally alive.

This is the completion of the universe and the completion of humankind. This is the rapture, the resurrection, and having received the seal. This is salvation, and it is to be born and live in the eternally living Heaven. This is to be born in and live in the Land of Truth while alive. One lives forever in this land, right here, with this body. This means the Jung (Spirit) and Shin (Soul), not the material land and the material body, live in this land (that has been reborn), right here. This world and the world of the afterlife are not separate but one and the same.

This world, which is the material world, disappears.
However, this world that is born in your mind is Truth
and eternally does not disappear.
The material world and body are one with the world and body
that is of the Holy Spirit and Holy Soul.
The people who are the masters of the world
save this forever-living, immortal world.
It is time for all to be saved and brought to life.
When it is time to live, we should all live.
The world before this world was born
was the universe emptiness.
The Spirit and Soul of this emptiness
is the omnipresent existence of the universe.
From here, the celestial bodies were born again in the universe.
Seen from the perspective of the emptiness that is the master,
everything in existence and nonexistence in this universe
all do not exist.
Only the Spirit and Soul exist.
Even though people are born on the earth,
they do not exist.
The earth also does not exist.
Neither the earth nor the people exist,
and the celestial bodies are also just the Spirit and Soul.
In the mind of a person who is the Spirit and Soul itself,
this world and people are born again.

Then the universe that is born again
inside this person's mind has become complete.
The masters of the Spirit and Soul of the universe
come as human beings and save this world,
create, give the seal, save humankind, resurrect,
and create the new world of Truth.
People live forever in this land, right here,
and it is Heaven, the Land of Bliss, and Paradise.
This land has become Paradise.
After being born in the true world,
you can see that the multitude of tales
that were told were all false.
All of them were lies.
A person who dreams false dreams
and does false deeds in the false world
knows neither what is false nor what is true.
But a person who is born in the true world
knows both Truth and falseness, so will live with wisdom.
The new Heaven and new earth is the Land of Truth,
and one who lives here is the one with wisdom.

THE HUMAN MIND IS THE UNIVERSE

The creators make the world born again within the person's mind, and this is the world in which one lives. The creators, who are the saviors, are also humans.

In the Bible, it says that humankind was created in the image of God because the mind that people made by taking pictures of the world is in the image of God, which is the world. This is also because the *Jung* (Spirit) and *Shin* (Soul) of the universe are one with the true mind of people. The human mind and the universe are one. Therefore, when a person discards the karma, habits, and body, which are the sins, the universe *Jung* and *Shin* remain within. This itself is his mind. He is one with the universe.

A person speaks and lives according to what he has in his mind. When Truth is within a person, one can know Truth. If born in the Land of Truth, he can know the Land of Truth. One can know as much as he has within. The one who has achieved it all is the one who is born in the true world and has the mind of the true world. Since the infinite universe is within, the *Jung* and *Shin* exist. This existence that is Truth is reborn, so this land, right here, is Paradise. It is Heaven, the Land of Bliss, Paradise.

THE LAND OF TRUTH

Truth is the existence of God, Buddha, Allah, *Haneolnim* (the word for God in an ancient Korean folk religion). Each religion gave Truth a different name. Christianity named it God, Buddhism named it Buddha, Islam named it Allah, and Koreans named it *Haneolnim*. This existence must exist inside a person's mind in order to exist—otherwise, it does not exist.

A person can only live when Truth and the Land of Truth exist within his mind. If it does not exist within him, it does not exist. Only the one who has the true world that is Truth within can live in that land.

It is the same for Heaven, the Land of Bliss, Paradise. One who has Heaven, the Land of Bliss, and Paradise, which is the Land of Truth, in his mind is the one who has gone there. One is born in this land only when he has gone to this land while living. One cannot go there if he does not have it within him because it does not exist. This is because the true world that is this world, and a person's mind, are one and the same.

When the self that is an illusion completely dies, the *Jung* (Spirit) and *Shin* (Soul), which are Truth, are within. And when the creators make you born anew in that land, this land, right here, is Heaven and Paradise. This land, right here, is the Land of Truth that eternally does not disappear; it exists within you.

WHAT WORK DOES TRUTH DO?

Truth is the *Jung* (Spirit) and *Shin* (Soul) of the infinite universe emptiness that exists in this world. This itself is a nonmaterial, real existence. The Soul exists within the emptiness where there is nothing. And the Spirit also exists. This existence does not disappear no matter how hard one tries to erase it. It does not disappear even if it is burned in a ten quadrillion degree fire. It is a place beyond the material. This existence is the source of all creations in the universe and is the material creator. All creations are born from this existence and return to it. Only when this existence becomes the creators of the Holy Spirit and Holy Soul can all creations in this world be saved.

First, the *Jung* and *Shin*, which are the creators, have to come in human form. Then the child of *Jung* and *Shin* has to come. This is the Trinity. This existence is the Way, the Truth, and the Life. This existence will have a person discard the karma, habits, and body, which is one's sin, and have him go to Truth. This world will then be created again in the mind of Truth, and Heaven and Paradise exist within. Only the one who is without sin can go there. Subsequently, one is a complete person and a person who has achieved it all. A person who is Truth makes everything become Truth.

THE INCOMPLETE WORLD

All creations in the universe that are born in this world are incomplete material forms that exist and then disappear. All of these material forms have never been born in this world and have never existed.

People who are illusions and who do not exist in the world say everything has been created; however, this is nothing but their delusions. All creations of this universe that have been born into this world were born through material creation by the *Jung* (Spirit) and *Shin* (Soul) of the emptiness. All creations of the universe in this world are incomplete, so they all exist and then disappear. It is the unintended will of the true Origin to carry out complete creation, which will make this universe become complete.

The true Origin does not have the mind that intends to or plans to do, yet it has the will. If all material creations were to vanish and disappear, there would be no meaning or purpose. All of these creations are the children of the creators and the creators themselves. There will be a time when they are made to exist and be saved.

Only the emptiness of the infinite universe existed in the place before all creations came forth. When seen from the perspective of the emptiness, even though the celestial bodies come forth in the sky that is born in this world, they have not been created. When seen from the Original Foundation, everything is the Soul and the Spirit. When seen from the human perspective, from the mind world that overlaps the world, it is said to have been created. However, that is the mind of a person who is living in the false world and thus does not exist. This is also why all creations that are born on the earth do not exist. From the perspective of the universe, everything that exists and does not exist is the same—none of them exist. That is why this world is not alive and therefore incomplete. For this world to be reborn as Truth and to become complete, it has to be born anew within a person's mind. When a person's mind becomes the *Jung* and *Shin* of the universe, which is Truth, and the mind is born again in that Land of *Jung* and *Shin*, that person will not disappear as he is Truth.

In the Bible, Buddhist scriptures, and in the Qur'an, it is said that God, Buddha, Allah are within the mind. It is also said that Heaven, the Land of Bliss, Paradise are within the mind.

Once the karma, habits, and body that are human sins and illusionary are eliminated, the masters of this world, the Spirit and Soul of the emptiness, remain. Everything is the Spirit and Soul, whether all creations exist or not. This is Truth. In Christianity, this is the God of the Holy Spirit and Holy Father. And this is the Buddha of the *Dharmakaya* and *Sambhogakaya*, and it is Allah. One can live only when there is absolutely no false self and when one becomes the Spirit and Soul.

Only the people who are the creators and the masters of the true world can save. This world can live eternally, for it is the world of Truth. It is Heaven, the Land of Bliss, and Paradise. One who does not have Heaven, the Land of Bliss, and Paradise within one's mind while living cannot go there. This land is the Land of Truth, which is this land, right here. This land is the Kingdom of God, Buddha, Allah.

In this world, there is no other existence that is more supreme and sacred than Truth. This is an eternal and never-changing entity, and it is a living entity.

When the material forms in this world are reborn as the entity of Truth, even after the material forms disappear, the Spirit and Soul, which is Truth, still exist as it is.

The infinite universe is the *Jung* and *Shin*. From the point of view of *Jung* and *Shin*, none of the celestial bodies in this world exist. This earth also does not exist when seen from the viewpoint of Truth. People do not exist because they live inside their own mind worlds. The things that are thought to exist or to have been created do not exist. This is because, instead of living in the world, a person lives in the illusory and false world, which is a copy of the world.

When seen from the viewpoint of the infinite universe, everything is nonexistent. All that is thought to exist in this world does not exist because those individual entities are the material forms that are not born in the true world. Whether the material forms exist or not, all is simply nothingness, which is the Spirit and Soul. Material entities only exist when born again as the *Jung* and *Shin* instead of the material form. Whatever is thought to exist only exists within human delusions.

If one looks at this world from the perspective of Truth, nothing has been created, nothing exists, and everything in existence and nonexistence are all the Spirit and Soul of the universe emptiness. Nothing can live forever until this world is created again and made to exist. Everything can live when the masters of the world come in shape and form, as human beings, and make them be born again. This is how something that does not exist is brought into existence. Creating something again is the rapture, for it is making it be born in the Land of Truth, which is the sky—then this world has ascended and gone to Heaven.

What was dead is brought to life, so this is the resurrection. It is to be marked with the seal. It is salvation. It is the redemption of humankind. It is the forever-living Heaven, the Land of Bliss, and Paradise. Because God, Buddha, and Allah, which are Truth, and also Heaven, the Land of Bliss, and Paradise are within your mind, falseness can be born in the true world, become Truth, and live forever. This is "achieving it all" and becoming complete. This is what it means to go from the nonexistent world to the existent world and to be born there. One lives because one has died.

EVERYTHING IS THE SPIRIT AND SOUL

When the self completely dies, only the Spirit and Soul remain. When there is no self at all, only the Spirit and Soul remain. When one's karma, habits, and body do not exist, only the Spirit and Soul remain, and one's mind becomes the Spirit and Soul of the infinite universe. The one who has become this Spirit and Soul will be born again through God's words, which are Truth. When this world and the self are told to be reborn, they are born again from within one's mind. Then they can live. The new Heaven and the new earth will exist in the human mind, and the human mind is the universe.

The human mind and the universe are not separate but one and the same. The universe is within you. All creations that have become Truth are within you. The Spirit and Soul of the infinite universe existed before you were born into the world and even before all the celestial bodies existed. Even when there are countless celestial bodies in this universe, it is the Spirit and Soul, which exist. Everything that exists and does not exist is simply the Spirit and Soul. The earth is also the Spirit and Soul.

Seen from the Original Foundation, all people, animals, and plants, which are born on earth, are the Spirit and Soul. Only humans, who do not live in the true world, think that this world has been created and that it exists. However, this is simply the perspective of humans, who are living in the mind world, which is a false world.

Seen from the Original Foundation, which is the source and Truth, everything that exists and does not exist is the Original Foundation. The creations in this world have never been born and are simply the Spirit and Soul, which is nothingness and Truth.

All creations have neither existed nor been created because the individual entities have not been born in the Land of Life. When the individual entity exists as a material form, it does not exist. That material form is incomplete because it only lives up to its material life span and then disappears. From the viewpoint of Truth, it does not exist.

THE SALVATION OF THE WORLD IS CARRIED OUT BY THE MASTERS OF THE WORLD WHO ARE HUMAN BEINGS

Each religion has prophesied the coming of *Maitreya* who is the savior, the coming of the Savior, the coming of *Jungdoryung* (the leader of righteous Truth), and *Daedoomok* (the great leader)— all of them have prophesied the coming of the entity who will save the world. It has been proclaimed that this entity, saints of salvation, will come—meaning that human beings will come. Only the masters of the world are able to save this world. In the era of incompletion, the Spirit and Soul of the universe brought forth all creations. Only when this Spirit and Soul come as human beings can the people and this world be saved within the human mind. This existence is the Way, the Truth, and the Life.

THE ERA OF COMPLETION

Having people throw away human sin, which is their karma, habits, and bodies, is the Way. The masters enable people to go to Truth and then make them be born again from there. Within the mind of a person who has been absolved of one's sins, only the Spirit and Soul, which is the universe mind, remains. When one is reborn from here through the words of this existence, this world and the self can be reborn and live in the Land of Truth that is within one's mind. This is how the nonexistent world is reborn, and the completion of the universe is achieved. This is creation, the rapture, being born as Truth, the resurrection, receiving the seal, salvation, and being born into and living in the eternally living Heaven. This land right here is born again within you, and this world and you live forever as Truth in this land, right here.

Now is the era of the completion of the universe, human completion, and the completion of the world and all creations. It is the era when everything in this world is resurrected and created again to live forever. The universe within the human mind that is Truth, and the universe in the true world are one. Everything in existence and nonexistence is the universe that has been born in this land, all of which has been born within one's self, and this self is now the master. All creations can exist because humans exist. The world where people are born as Truth exists, and so people are the masters. Because people exist, everything that exists and does not exist in the world also exists. The world exists because people exist, and without people, there is no meaning or purpose to the world, even if it does exist.

It is now the era of the completion of the universe. At this time, one who is absolved of all the sins of one's false self can live eternally without dying. Everything is alive in the land of completion. A person who lives in that land always lives there regardless of whether one's body is alive or dead. Everything in this world would be a dream for that person. The one who does not have the complete world within the mind while living will not be able to live.

IT MUST EXIST WITHIN YOUR MIND FOR IT TO EXIST

God and God's Kingdom are within you. If God and God's Kingdom are not inside a person's mind, one is not alive because one is not in God's world. If Truth does not exist within your mind, it does not exist. Truth must exist within your mind for it to exist.

For a person who lives inside the world of sin, which is the self-created mind world, the world does not exist when he dies. Neither the sinner nor the world exists. When the sinner and the sinner's false world entirely disappear, Truth appears. This Truth is the Spirit and Soul of the emptiness.

Since one's false self and world do not exist,
only the Spirit and Soul, which are Truth, exist.
This itself is one's mind.
When neither the false self nor the world exist,
the Spirit and Soul, which is Truth, remains.
From here, the people who are the masters of Truth
bring forth rebirth to this world and one's self.
Then, the self and the true world
are born again in the Land of Truth that is "within you."
Everything exists within one's mind.
When one closes his eyes, the Original Foundation exists,
and when he opens his eyes, the world exists.
It all exists "within you."
In the false world, one knew nothing
and had unresolved questions, doubts, suffering, and burdens.
But in the new world,

there are no unresolved questions, doubts, suffering, or burdens. It is the land of freedom and liberation where everything is alive. One is at ultimate rest, and he is free from everything because his false self does not exist.
All the fixed conceptions, habits, and customs
that one had when he was a human being have disappeared. One sees things just the way they are, and one just lives.

THE ERA OF THE CREATION OF THE HOLY SPIRIT AND HOLY SOUL

To live, or to die? That is *the* question. When people die after living in this world, what they have in their minds will determine whether they will live or die. One who has only the life lived, which is the false mind, within one's mind will not be able to think or have consciousness when he dies.

A dead person cannot cry out in pain even if stabbed. After living with only false minds, when one dies, even that falseness disappears. Therefore, when one dies, only the corpse will remain, and once it gets burned, there will be nothing.

A person who has the karma, habits, and body inside one's mind, which is human sin, cannot live unless he is absolved of that sin. A person who has been absolved of his sins has Truth within him. For this person, the world and one's self are born in the Land of Truth and this person is still alive even when his physical body dies. This is because even if one's self disappears, one's self and this world that is reborn from within one's mind are still alive as they are because they have been born as Truth. So whether one is alive or dead, it is one and the same. Even after the material self disappears, he just exists. He lives forever in this land, right here.

During the era of the creation of the Holy Spirit and Holy Soul, all things are created as the *Jung* (Spirit) and *Shin* (Soul), so it is the era of the completion of the universe, human completion, and the completion of all creations. The Spirit and Soul of the universe emptiness brought about material creation. Creation of the Holy Spirit and Holy Soul can only be carried out when the existence of the Spirit and Soul, which is Truth, comes as human beings.

This world has never been created until now; everything was just the nothingness of the Spirit and Soul. However, all creations that exist in this infinite universe have been reborn within the mind of a person who has become Truth. Since one has been created anew, he has been saved, resurrected, marked with a seal, and raptured. It is time to reach and live in the eternally living Heaven while living. The creation of the Holy Spirit and Holy Soul is the complete creation.

IT IS NOW TIME FOR HUMAN COMPLETION

Human completion is when people are eternally alive without death. For a person to become complete, one needs to discard one's sin, which is karma, habits, and body. Only the emptiness itself, which is the *Jung* (Spirit) and *Shin* (Soul), will remain in one's mind. This existence is Truth. One's false self has died, and only Truth remains within. From there, the ones who are the masters of the true world create again within your mind. This world and your self are then born again from inside your mind and this land, right here, is the world of your mind. This world is indestructible. It is Truth, and it just exists as it is.

IS REINCARNATION REAL OR NOT?

People commonly believe that our physical bodies reincarnate when we die. There are also many people who believe that when we die, we go to some other world. When a person dies, there is nothing. When incomplete material forms are created and then disappear, nothing remains.

In Buddhism, it says that everything comes from the earth, water, fire, and wind, and then everything scatters back to the earth, water, fire, and wind. Christianity says that only a pile of earth remains. However, it is the way of the world, and a matter of course, that nothing remains when material substances disappear. All material forms that are born in this world come from the Original Foundation and go back to this Original Foundation. Everything that is born in this material world lives up to its life span and then disappears.

According to Christianity, those who believe in Jesus Christ will go to Heaven when they die, and those who do not believe will go to hell. Buddhism says that those who do good deeds will go to Paradise, while those who do bad deeds will go to hell. These words mean that in the time of the creation of the Holy Spirit and Holy Soul, when one discards his sin, which is the karma, habits, and body, his mind becomes Truth. From there, when one is reborn by the words of Truth's masters, that place is Heaven. Only when Truth and the Land of Truth exist within oneself can he live in Heaven. Paradise is the same; when one discards one's sin, which is karma, habits, and body, he can enlighten to all four virtues of the *Nirvana Sutra: nitya* (eternal permanence), *sukha* (bliss), *atman* (true self), and *suddha* (purity).

Regardless of which belief system it is, they all say that when the saint who saves the world comes as a human being, rebirth can be carried out. When one's mind becomes Truth, the saviors will save the entire world of Truth within one's mind. This is creation, the resurrection, Ascension, having received the seal, and eternal life in Heaven and Paradise.

THE METHOD FOR PEOPLE NOT TO DIE

People are born into this world with their bodies, and when their bodies disappear, they disappear.

Just as the *Jung* (Spirit) and *Shin* (Soul) of the universe created all material entities in this world, when the *Jung* and *Shin* itself come as human beings, only then can the creation of the Holy Spirit and Holy Soul take place. When it does, this existence will eliminate people's karma, habits, and body, which are the sins, from their minds and make their minds become the true mind.

Creation of the Holy Spirit and Holy Soul is when the masters of the world create the world and one's self from this true mind so that one can live forever.

Nothing in this world has ever been created; it is simply the human mind that thinks things exist or do not exist. It is a false mind that humans have made. Everything is *Jung* and *Shin* from the viewpoint of Truth. When the masters of the world make one's mind become Truth and enable one to be reborn through their words, all creations in this world can be born again as Truth and live. This is the only way not to die. The way for people not to die is to be born again as Truth from this world, which is Truth. Truth can become one's mind only for those who have discarded one's karma, habits, and body, which are his sins. And only then can they be born again and live.

Now is the time when one can live forever. Only those who repent will be able to live. In order to live, the self who is living in one's false mind world has to disappear and then has to be born again in the true world.

THE WAY FOR A PERSON TO GO TO HEAVEN, THE TRUE WORLD

The reason why people are incomplete is that, rather than being one with the mind of the world, they are living inside their own mind worlds, which overlap the world. People do not have Heaven, which is Truth, in their minds. Instead, they have their karma, habits, and body in their minds—this is why people have falseness in their minds. Once a person discards this, Heaven, which is Truth, exists within one's mind. When one is born again from there, he is a person who has gone to Heaven.

When the masters, who are Truth, come to this world, they are the Way, the Truth, and the Life. They will have people cleanse their karma, habits, and bodies. And when one's mind becomes Truth, the masters will create the true world in that true mind. This itself is the rapture, the resurrection, salvation, and being marked with the seal. It is to be born into and live in the eternally living Heaven. Unless one goes to the Land of Truth and is born there while they are alive, they will end up simply dying when they die.

EVERYTHING THAT PEOPLE BELIEVE EXISTS, ACTUALLY DOES NOT EXIST

People live in false worlds because the world exists inside their human minds, which are illusions. Everything that people believe exists actually does not exist. Anything that people say is false. Before the arrival of Truth, everything that was thought to exist actually did not exist. Nothing has ever existed in this world. Thinking that it exists is the false human mind. When a false person completely dies, only the mind of Truth remains, and when a person is born again in that Land of Truth, that is when he exists and has actually been created.

ONLY THAT WHICH EXISTS INSIDE THE MIND THAT HAS BECOME TRUTH EXISTS

The nonexistent world must transform into the existent world. The world is said to be nonexistent because it does not exist inside people's minds. It does not exist because people are living in illusionary worlds.

From the viewpoint of Truth, this world has never been born, nor has it been created. It is only humans, who are illusory, who think that the world exists. This world does not exist from the perspective of the universe, which is Truth. This world has never been born, and it has never been created. Only the human mind thinks that it exists. For this world to exist, it has to be created in the mind of a person who has become Truth. The only things that exist are that which exist in the mind that has become Truth.

WHAT IS TRUE CREATION? THE EXISTENCE OF SAVIORS IS NEITHER WITHIN A NAME NOR IN A RELIGION

God and God's Kingdom are within the mind. When a person who is false completely dies and the Original Foundation, which is the source, becomes one's mind, the creators create this world again. Then this world is born again inside one's self. It becomes the Land of Truth that lives forever and never dies. The place you are living right now—this land, right here, is born again from within your mind. Therefore it is Truth and is eternally alive.

This land is God's, Buddha's, and Allah's land that is the Land of Truth. The ultimate purpose is for all to go to this land and live there. This land lives because it is the Land of Truth. The reason and purpose why humans are born into and live in this world is to go to this land. The ultimate purpose of each religion is also to go to this land and live there. What has no death and lives eternally is the energy and light of the universe itself, which is Truth. All creations in the universe are born from here and live forever in this land, right here.

Throughout the world, people say that the Savior, the Second Coming of Christ, *Maitreya*, *Jungdoryung* (the leader of righteous Truth), or *Daedoomok* (the great leader) will come and save the world. And in each religion, it is thought and believed that such an existence will come from one's own religion. However, people in this world cannot know the existence that takes them to the Land of Truth. It does not exist in a name, nor does it exist in religion. If there is a place that takes you to the Land of Truth, wouldn't that place be the real one? It is not that the name must be the Second Coming of Christ, *Maitreya*, *Jungdoryung*, or

Daedoomok. And it is not that the religion must be Christianity, Buddhism, or Islam. Whoever takes you to the Land of Truth would be Truth. Wouldn't the place where you can achieve the ultimate purpose of humankind and the ultimate purpose of religion be the real one?

In each religious scripture, it says that the savior will come from outside the conventional norm. Only the ones who take people to the Land of Truth that is within their minds would be the real ones. It was said that one should not believe that Buddha, Allah, and God exist in a certain place here or there. God, Buddha, Allah exist within you, and the land of God, Buddha, Allah also exists within you.

This place is the Land of Truth, and it is also Truth. Anything that is not Truth must all be false. Only Truth would be real and true. This land is a place where people need to go while they are alive. This land is without life or death, a land of oneness. There are no unresolved questions or doubts, and it is the land of liberation that is free from everything. Only the one who has been born in this land has achieved human completion and is an existence that is born and living in the land of the complete universe. The existence that takes people to this land, regardless of the name, exists neither in a name nor in religion.

In each religious prophecy, it is said that this existence will come from outside the conventional norm. This means that it exists neither in a particular name nor does it exist in religion. The ones who take people to the Land of Truth and enable them to be born again would be the real ones. To find this real existence, one should go to the place that takes them to the Land of Truth. And then, one should find the existence of Truth inside one's mind. If there is someone who takes you to the Land of Truth that is within your mind, this existence must be the real one.

Only this true existence is the Way, the Truth, and the Life that can take people to the Land of Truth. This existence is the masters of the world and Truth and, therefore, can save the world and all of humanity. Through their words, everything in this world can be created. Unless one is born again through the words, there is no one who can live. In this world, when the universe without shape or form was the master, everything in existence and nonexistence was just nothingness, the Original Foundation. All creations in this world have neither ever been born nor have they ever existed. Only humans who are living in the illusionary worlds were saying that they themselves exist and that they themselves have been created.

When one's false karma, habits, and body completely die, one is born again in the Land of Truth. And when you see from the Original Foundation, which is Truth, nothing has ever existed. When the emptiness was the master, it was a world where there was nothing. When this existence that is Truth comes as human beings, this world and people are born again in the true world in people's minds. Then, they exist. This world that is created again can exist because people exist.

One lives forever in this land, right here. Creation is done by the people who are the masters of the world that have come in shape and form. When told to be born again, the world and one's self can be born again within and can live eternally. This existence, which is the creators, creates this world. The creators save everything by creating again from nothingness. Unless something is born in the true world, it does not exist. Only what exists in one's mind exists.

If it does not exist in one's mind, it does not exist. What exists is the world that has been born again within your mind. This land right here becomes your mind, and this world that is born through the words of the creators is alive without death. This land exists because it is Truth. This land is Truth and is eternally alive within you. This is the completion of this world, the completion of the universe, and human completion. Only this is true creation. Only what is born in this land has been created.

PART 2

THE ROADMAP TO FINDING TRUTH WITHIN

Just as we use a GPS to navigate from our current location to our desired destination, now we have a navigation system to find Truth within while we are alive.

GOD, BUDDHA, ALLAH, *HANEOLNIM*, AND HEAVEN, THE LAND OF BLISS, PARADISE, THE LAND OF *HANEOLNIM* ARE WITHIN YOU

Humans live only speaking and behaving according to what they have in their minds. Humans are sinners because they are the cameras that with their eyes, noses, ears, mouths, and bodies take pictures of what belongs to the world and of the events that happened throughout their lives. These pictures are not real; they are not real because the film exist in their minds.

Since people live being dictated by this falseness, they dream false dreams and do false things in a false world. As people have only falseness in their minds, God, Buddha, Allah, and the world of those entities do not exist in their minds. When God, Heaven and Paradise exist within a person's mind, he is able to know God, be born in Heaven, and live.

Only the one who has gone to this Kingdom while living has that Kingdom, and thus, is able to live eternally. This is why when the life lived, which is the karma, along with the habits inherited from one's parents are eliminated, one returns to the Original Foundation, which is the Origin and Truth. When you are born from there, God, Buddha, Allah exist in your mind, and Heaven, the Land of Bliss, Paradise and the Land of Divine Beings always exist in your mind. So you can live there eternally while you are alive. One who does not have this true world in one's mind at all times will not be able to go there.

It is not such that one goes to Heaven, the Land of Bliss, Paradise, the Land of Divine Beings after this physical body dies. Instead, what one must do is go to Heaven, Paradise, the Land of Divine Beings while alive. God, Buddha, Allah and Haneolnim must exist within you at all times, and that Land, which is Truth, must exist within you.

The reason why a person cannot go to this Land of Truth and does not have Truth and the Land of Truth is that he lives inside the mind of his self, who is neither a saint nor a righteous person. Having discarded his false self, which is not real, one who has the true world, which is Truth and true, is a saint and a righteous person.

WHAT HAPPENS WHEN A PERSON DIES? HOW CAN A PERSON LIVE ETERNALLY?

When someone dies, we think that this person goes to the world beyond and lives there. However, there is nothing when a person dies. Death means for life to disappear. When life disappears, the body, mind, thoughts, and everything that existed while one was alive also disappear.

Let us suppose there is a dead person next to you. This person is dead, so he cannot think. Even if this person is stabbed, he would not be able to cry out in pain. He would not know even if his entire body is eliminated. All that once existed would no longer exist. When this existence is burned and has disappeared in a fire, nothing will remain.

Every material entity in this world lives only once, and there is no afterlife. However, if the falseness completely dies and then is born anew, is reborn and resurrected, one can live eternally. Only the one who has gone to the Kingdom of God and Buddha, while living, and has been born again can live in the eternally living Heaven. The way to live forever is to repent. And only the place where you become true is the place of Truth. If you cannot become Truth, it would all be false.

THE REASON WHY PEOPLE COULD NOT BECOME COMPLETE AND TRUE UNTIL NOW IS BECAUSE THE METHOD DID NOT EXIST

The reason why humans are incomplete is that they have turned their backs on the world, which is Truth. With the things of the world, a person has made his own mind world and has been living inside of it.

Scientists estimate that about 70 trillion people have come and gone. However, there was no method for discovering Truth because people lived inside their minds, false worlds, and could not see from the perspective of the world. But when there are people who see from the perspective of the world, those people would know that humans are living in false worlds with suffering and burden. Those people would also know that people are living inside nonexistent worlds, false worlds. Through wisdom, they would know all the principles of the world. Also, it would be the same for the method for human completion.

When the existence of Truth comes as human beings, those people can know the method because they have wisdom. People who are real and Truth would have the method to enable incomplete people to discard the karma, habits, and body, become the mind of the world, and then be born again.

A PERSON WHO IS FALSE CANNOT BECOME TRUTH UNLESS HE REPENTS

If falseness is to become Truth, falseness must be discarded and be reborn from Truth.

WHAT IS ENLIGHTENMENT?

Enlightenment is what one comes to know as much as one has become Truth by cleansing his false mind.

In the Bible, it says that a person believes with his heart and confesses with his mouth in order to be saved. One has enlightened to this verse if his mind enlightens and realizes, "Ah, this is what it means." For falseness to become Truth, one can enlighten to the degree that the false mind is discarded. Thus, you must enlighten profusely until you become complete.

OMNISCIENCE AND OMNIPOTENCE

In the Bible, it says that knowing God is the source of wisdom. The reason why there is nothing that humans know is that they live possessing only their individual experiences. Therefore, there is no Truth or wisdom in their minds.

The infinite universe is the emptiness that exists within all creations. This universe itself is God, Buddha, Allah, *Haneolnim* (the word for God in an ancient Korean folk religion). When your mind has become this existence, and you are born again, you can know all the principles of the world. All creations of this world are born from this existence, which is omnipotent. This universe emptiness itself is the Origin, which is Truth, and it has created all creations.

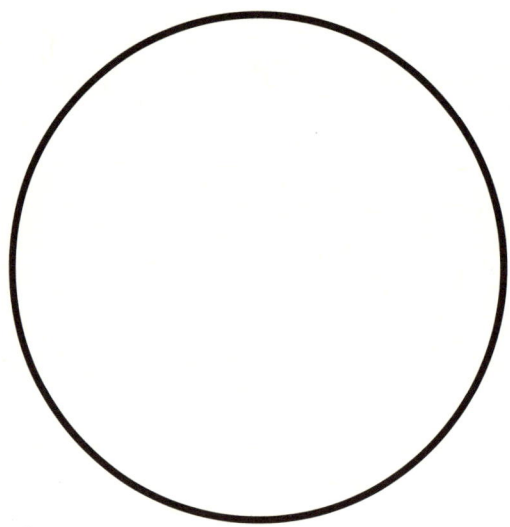

Universe Emptiness

Because all creations are born from here, it is omnipotent. When this existence of Truth comes in physical form as true people, this world and humankind can be saved.

HOW CAN ONE BE ABSOLVED OF ONE'S SINS, EXTINGUISH ONE'S KARMA, AND PRACTICE REPENTANCE AND PENITENCE?

Jesus Christ said, "I am the Way, the Truth, and the Life." The method of repentance, penitence, extinguishing your karma, and being absolved of your sins is the Way. In this world, people could not become saints or righteous people because there was no method to do so. This method can only come to be when the existence of Truth comes to this world as human beings.

People are sinners because they are living in the false world, and because they live having turned their backs on Truth, which is the world. The reason why there is not a single righteous person among people is because the karma, habits, and this body itself are illusory and false. To discard the karma:

1. Discard the remembered thoughts.
2. Discard the images of the self and the images of the relationships.
3. Discard the body.
4. Discard the body and the universe.
5. Discard the body and the universe.
6. The self disappears and becomes the universe.
7. Eliminate the false world and the self.

For the habits, when one eliminates one's body, the habits that are inside the body are revealed, and can then be discarded. When one eliminates one's body, only this world remains. When one's mind becomes the true world, one can see and know God, Buddha, Allah, *Haneolnim*. When one is reborn in this land, one can be born in Heaven and live. When the self that is not real is eliminated, one can achieve human completion.

THE REASON AND PURPOSE WHY HUMANS ARE BORN INTO THIS WORLD

The reason and purpose why humans are born into this world is so they can achieve human completion and live eternally.

According to some scientists, humans first appeared on earth seven million years ago. It is said that God created man in his own image. The reason why humans were said to be created in the image of God is because God is the world, and they took pictures of the things of this world and then stored them inside their human mind worlds.

The minds that humans have are the individualistic minds, and people think that they "know" things based on the pictures that they have taken of their experiences. With these self-centered minds, they live believing that only they are correct. These are false lives, lived in false worlds.

When a person dies, there is nothing. As this life of incompletion continued, there have been countless wars, and people struggled for their own countries, to make everything theirs. It is the will of the masters of Truth to save humankind when this world is fully populated with people. In this way, more people can be saved.

The reason why people are incomplete is that they live inside the worlds of their minds. When people eliminate these incomplete mind worlds and are born again with the mind world of the universe that is Truth and real, they can become complete. If humans had been made complete from the beginning, they would not have been motivated to marry, and humankind would have become extinct from this world. Now is the time of harvest; it is time to save humankind and the world and make them live inside the mind of a person who has become Truth.

The salvation that people have long been waiting for begins when the population of this world is filled to capacity. The reason and purpose humans are born into this world is to be reborn into the true world.

ONE WHO HAS TRUTH IN ONE'S MIND CAN KNOW BOTH TRUTH AND FALSENESS

God, Buddha, Allah, *Haneolnim* (the word for God in an ancient Korean folk religion) are all the existence of Truth. Heaven, the Land of Bliss, Paradise, the Land of *Haneolnim* are the Land of Truth. When there is no false self in the world, your mind becomes the true world. Then, you can see and know the existence of Truth, which is God, Buddha, Allah, *Haneolnim*.

The resurrection and rapture are when one's mind becomes this existence, Truth, and one is born again. From this world, when you eliminate the human mind world, which overlaps the true world,

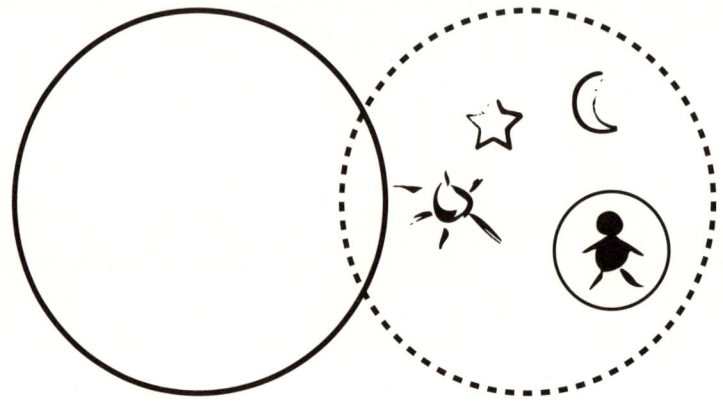

the universe, which is real and Truth, becomes your mind.

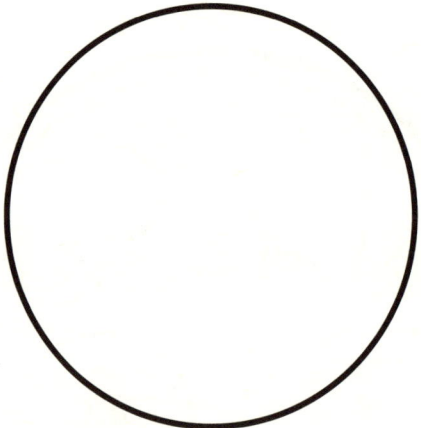

Truth can be known when it exists inside one's mind. One who has the real Truth within one's mind knows both Truth and falseness. But the one who lives in the false world knows neither Truth nor falseness.

WHAT ARE HERESIES AND CULTS?

Heresies and cults are what are fake. If the place a person is attending is real, one should have become Truth. If one has not become complete and true, it would mean the place that one is attending is false. One could claim that only what he has is right and what others have is false, but then it would be nothing more than his own opinion. If what one has is right, then one should have become Truth.

Now is the era when anyone can become Truth. When one erases the false things one has from one's mind and eliminates the self, one can become Truth. All the places, which only talk about Truth instead of becoming the real Truth, are all not real. A place is only real when one becomes Truth.

SALVATION

In each religion, it is often said that when the Savior comes, salvation will come to pass. It is also stated that when the *Maitreya* comes, there will be salvation. In Korea, it is said that when *Jungdoryung* (the leader of righteous Truth) comes, salvation will be possible. It was also prophesied that *Daedoomok* (the great leader) would come. All of these entities are Truth, and these mean that the existence of Truth will come to the world and will come as human beings. As these existences are the masters of the world, the world will be changed to become the world of Truth—this is salvation. Salvation is making falseness be born again as Truth in the Land of Truth. It is to discard the false human mind world and to make the true world exist within people's minds. It is to save people by making the world born anew and resurrected as Truth. This world can be saved because it exists inside the human mind, and the masters who have come as human beings are the masters. Within that mind world, the world exists, and the one who has been saved is the king and the master.

THE END OF THE WORLD

People often think that during the end times, "the end of the world" will occur through infectious diseases, starvation, earthquakes, and wars. However, these have always existed since humankind started living on earth.

For a person who is living in the false world, it will be the end of the world because he is not born in the true world. There is no end of the world for a person who is born in the true world.

The way to repent and become Truth is to discard your self that is false and not real. One who has become Truth is an immortal who lives in this land, right here, for eternity. This existence is the one who has become the Holy Son, Buddha, a Divine Being, and God.

The end of the world does not exist for a complete person, but it exists for a person who has not become complete. If one is not born again, it is simply the end—it is the end of the world.

THE RAPTURE AND THE RESURRECTION

The rapture is to ascend into the air, and resurrection is to come back to life. There was a time when the Damisun Church talked about the rapture taking place, and it became a widely discussed issue.

There have also been numerous other talks about the rapture and that only the ones who receive the seal will live, and only 144,000 people will live, etc. However, none of those prophecies have come true until now, which means they are all false. Any prophecies that made predictions about certain dates have never been correct. The story of only 144,000 people being saved and becoming complete is also false unless it actually comes true.

No one can be born into Truth unless one eliminates one's sin and karma and is reborn as Truth. There must be a method for falseness to become Truth. For anyone to be reborn in Truth, which is the land of completion, only the one who knows and believes in the will of Truth can be reborn and achieve it. Those who try to achieve it without repenting will not be able to achieve. This also applies to the rapture and the resurrection. When you throw away the picture world, which is a false world in your mind, Heaven, which is the true world, becomes your mind. When you are born from there, you are born in Heaven and have been raptured, and to be born again is the resurrection. Although they are two different words, rapture and resurrection both mean to go from the false world to the true world.

THE EXISTENCE THAT CAN GIVE SALVATION

Salvation is to take people from the false world and have them be born in the true world. Since only the people of the true world can take people who are in the false world, people can be saved only when the people of the true world come.

REPENTANCE

Repentance is to discard the false human karma, habits, and body. When the false conceptions, habits, customs, and self that a human has does not exist, one can be born as Truth. When one is reborn from there, one can become Truth and become an eternally living immortal.

Repentance is to subtract one's karma, habits, and body from the world. Then one can know all the principles of the world.

People are incomplete because they live inside the human mind world. Completion is to become the mind of the world and be born into that world.

WHEN EVERYONE BECOMES COMPLETE AND TRUE, RELIGIONS, PHILOSOPHIES, IDEOLOGIES, EDUCATION, POLITICS, AND ECONOMIES WILL BECOME ONE

Religions, philosophies, ideologies, education, politics, and economies all exist inside people's minds. Each person has different opinions about these topics because people's minds are different. When one's mind becomes the real Truth, the world and all people will become one. This is what is real.

Previously it was an era when people only talked about Truth. Now, people will act from Truth and they will live well because there will be results.

HOW TO SEE AND KNOW GOD, BUDDHA, ALLAH, *HANEOLNIM*

The way to see and know God, Buddha, Allah, *Haneolnim* (God from an ancient Korean folk religion) is for one's self who is a sinner to completely die and disappear. Then, God, Buddha, Allah, *Haneolnim* that are the existence of Truth, which exists within one's mind, can be seen and known. Just as people cannot know what they do not have in their minds, only a saint and a righteous person can know this. Only the one whose mind has become Truth can know.

HOW TO GO TO HEAVEN, THE LAND OF BLISS, PARADISE, THE LAND OF DIVINE BEINGS

The way to go to Heaven, the Land of Bliss, Paradise, the Land of Divine Beings is for the false self to completely die and disappear and become the mind of the universe, which is Truth. Then the world and oneself that is reborn from there has Heaven, the Land of Bliss, Paradise, the Land of the Divine Beings within one's mind, and one will always live in that Land. This is how one can live there.

THE SHAPE AND FORM OF GOD, BUDDHA, ALLAH, *HANEOLNIM*

Just as humans have bodies and minds, this infinite universe also has a body and mind. People cannot see this existence because this existence does not exist in people's minds. It seems as if there is nothing in this universe emptiness. However, this existence is a non-material, real existence. It has no shape or form, and there is nothing in it. But, the Holy Spirit and Holy Soul, which are the universe body and mind, exist within. This existence is the omniscient and omnipotent Origin that has created all creations. This existence is Truth. It is an existence of Truth that does not disappear in a fire or under any other circumstances. This existence is the omniscient and omnipotent God, Buddha, Allah, *Haneolnim* (God from an ancient Korean folk religion).

Salvation is to be reborn in this land, which is Truth. Everything that is born in this world is the shape and form of God, Buddha, Allah, *Haneolnim*. Those that are born in the world of Truth become eternally living immortals and have no death.

TO BE REBORN AND RESURRECTED

To be reborn and resurrected means for the falseness to be born as Truth. The world and people that exist in the false human mind have to be reborn and resurrected in the true world in order to live.

FOR HUMANS TO BE BORN, WE NEED TO HAVE PARENTS. LIKEWISE, FOR PEOPLE TO BE BORN AS TRUTH, WE NEED TO HAVE PARENTS OF TRUTH

One can be resurrected as Truth by the words of the parents of Truth. Since those words are life, they can create the world and people anew in an individual's mind. This is what it means to truly live. One can be born again by the words of the masters. The everlasting Heaven belongs to the person who has gone to that true Kingdom. A person who does not have this Kingdom will simply end up dying.

THE BIBLE, BUDDHIST SUTRAS, *JEUNGSANDOJEON*, AND *WON BUDDHIST SUTRAS*

All the holy scriptures are prophecy books about the era of completion. In the Bible, it says that Jesus, who is Truth, will return. In the Buddhist sutras, it says that *Maitreya* will come to save mankind. *JeungSanDoJeon* (sacred text of the Korean religion *Jeung San Do*) says that *Maitreya*, who is the Great Leader, will come, and the *Won Buddhist Sutras* also spoke of the coming of *Maitreya*. All of these mean that people who are false will become Truth, be reborn as the eternally living Truth, and be saved.

In the past, it was not the time of completion; the scriptures were prophecies for people to become complete and live when that time comes.

ARE YOU BECOMING REAL IN THE PLACE YOU ARE ATTENDING RIGHT NOW?

Heresy refers to a place of falseness. However, any place that is not true is all false.

One has to reflect and ask oneself:
- In this place that I am attending, am I becoming Truth?
- Am I achieving human completion?
- Am I living in Heaven forever, right now?

If not, that place is false. One should eliminate one's conceptions, habits and customs regarding what is heresy and false; and then eliminate the self. Thereafter, one can go to the Land of God, Buddha, Allah and be born there. This place is the Land of Truth.

Let us all repent, be absolved of our sins, be born in the true world, and live eternally.

One sees others as heretics because one has heresy within. Heretics call others heresies. It is all heresy and false unless one has become complete.

WHEN THE TIME TO BECOME COMPLETE TRUTH COMES, WHERE YOU CAN BECOME TRUTH IS THE PLACE OF COMPLETION

Many people believe that in the second coming of Christ, the same Jesus who passed away 2,000 years ago will return with the same appearance. However, Jesus does not dwell in his outward appearance—when Truth comes in the minds of human beings, then Jesus Christ has come.

Salvation can take place when the masters of the world come as human beings. It is the same with *Maitreya*. *Maitreya* has come when people who have the mind of Truth, the mind of the world, come.

THE ERA OF THE WAY, THE TRUTH, AND THE LIFE

Only the masters of the world can take people to the true world and have them be born there. Therefore they are the Way and also the masters of the world. Because they can give life, they are Truth and life.

THE ERA WHEN EVERYONE CAN BECOME A DIVINE BEING, SAINT, AND BUDDHA

When one's body and mind, which are false, disappear, one goes back to Truth, which is the Origin. Then, anyone can become a Divine Being, saint, and Buddha if they are born again from the Origin.

ONE WHO THROWS HIMSELF AWAY TO FIND TRUTH WILL FIND JESUS, BUDDHA, AND THE DIVINE BEING

Those who are looking for the Jesus, Buddha and Divine Beings of the past will never find Jesus, Buddha or Divine Beings. The entity of Truth, which is real, does not exist in the shape or the outward appearance—it exists in the mind. So, people will not be able to recognize these entities even if they exist. The Jesus, Buddha and Divine Beings that people are expecting will not come. Therefore, people do not know even when these existences have come. People cannot recognize the people of Truth because they seek Truth in the outward appearance.

HOW TO GO FROM INCOMPLETION TO COMPLETION

To go from incompletion to completion, it is necessary for a person's mind to become Truth by repenting; repentance is eliminating what is incomplete. There is Heaven, Paradise, the Land of Divine Beings within you when you are born from there.

DO WE LIVE FOREVER WITH THIS BODY?

The Bible says that one will live forever with "this body" in this land, right here, as it is. But "this body" indicates the body of the Holy Spirit and Holy Soul. The material body cannot live forever, and it disappears if destroyed or burned in a fire. In this world, there is nothing of material substance that lasts forever. This body can only live up to its life span. Only the Spirit and Soul, which is born as Truth, in the shape of this body, lives forever. This is why the Bible says one will live forever with this body. This land, right here, is born as Truth. The world where one is born with this body is Truth, and this body that is born as Truth can live forever in this land, right here.

UNION WITH GOD

When people think of God, they usually think that this existence exists as an individual entity. However, the infinite emptiness of the universe itself is God. This itself is the Spirit and Soul, *Jung* and *Shin*. This existence is a living God, and all creations are representations of this Spirit and Soul. When this existence comes in human form, it is possible to make people become one with God. At this time, people are resurrected again when they go back to the Origin through repentance, which is the absolution of sin. Then, the Spirit and this body become one by the words of this existence. This is a union with God.

Of course, to become one with God means the Spirit and Soul, which is born by the words of this existence, is one and the same as one's body. The masters of the original universe, who are the Holy Spirit, Holy Soul and Holy Son, are born on their own from the mind of the universe itself. This is the resurrection and rapture.

The place where one is reborn and lives is Heaven, which is Truth, and one lives there forever. Even after this body disappears, the Spirit and Soul that was one with the physical body lives without death in this land, right here, which is Heaven. This land right here, which is born as Truth, and the body of the Spirit and Soul, which is reborn as Truth, live forever.

THE DIFFERENCE BETWEEN THE PEOPLE WHO ARE POSSESSED AND THE PEOPLE WHO SPOKE OF TRUTH AND PROPHESIED THE COMING OF TRUTH

The so-called fortune tellers speak as if they know things and make predictions based on what they heard from the *Spirit of the Mountain*, *The Great Jade Emperor*, or some other gods in their minds. These are all manifestations of their false selves, and these come from the sense of inferiority in their mind worlds. Whether such predictions were correct or not, either way, they do not exist. These words are incorrect because they come from one's delusional thoughts.

The prophets who wrote books such as the Bible, Buddhist scriptures, and various Korean scriptures and prophetic books such as *The Scriptures of Won Buddhism*, *JeungSanDojeon*, *PalGongDoIn*, *Gyeogam Yurok*, and *JungGamRok*, could prophesy Truth because in that moment, they were reborn as the Spirit and Soul of Prophecies, so they were able to see the universe itself, which is Truth.

This is also why they could prophesy the future coming of the masters of Truth and when it will take place. It is the same for a complete person: one goes to the mind of the universe itself, and then one's self, who is Truth, is born from there.

TRUTH

The emptiness itself of the entire universe is the original Truth.

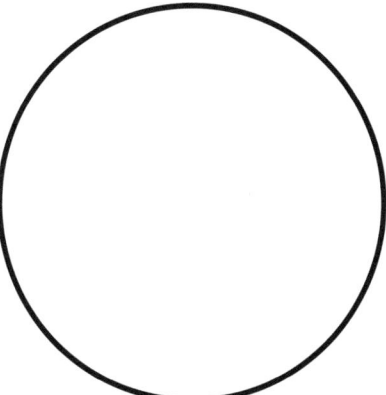

Truth is also the world where the world and people are born again in the Land of Truth. This is created by the existence of Truth that has come as human beings.

FAITH

Faith is to become one. Christianity says that if you believe in Jesus, you will go to Heaven. Believing in Jesus means that your mind has become one with Jesus. The mind of Jesus is Truth, which is this world. Since Jesus died on the cross in this world, the mind of Jesus became the true world and he was resurrected from there. So, he is one who is born in the Land of Truth.

In order to become a righteous person or a saint, people must also die like Jesus in order to reach righteousness. Only then can one go to the eternally living Heaven while living. To believe in Jesus means that you have become Truth and have been born again in the Land of Truth.

CREATION

Only the masters of the world can create. In the human mind world, it is thought that the celestial bodies and all things in this world have been created. But when seen from the standpoint of the universe, which is Truth, nothing has ever been created.

Existence and nonexistence are one—they are both the universe emptiness itself, which is nothingness. When seen from the perspective of the universe emptiness that is the creator, there is no mind that something exists. So existence and nonexistence are one and the same.

True creation happens when the masters of the world come as human beings. This existence will eliminate all of people's sin and karma, make people become the universe mind that is Truth, and from there will create the world and people through the words. Each individual will then have the Kingdom of the Universe inside one's mind, so people become the masters and the kings. Making people be born as Truth is true creation.

The creation in which the material forms exist in this world and then disappear is not God's will.

The era in which people are the masters is the era of human completion. This land, right here, is Heaven, the Land of Bliss, Paradise, and it is the era of Divine Beings. All religions will become one. The world will become one big country where there is no distinction between "your country" and "my country." Although each person has a different mind, when one's mind becomes the mind of the world, which is Truth, all the people of the world become one. Then all religions, philosophies, ideologies, academics, and sciences will become one and thus become righteous.

A COMPLETE PERSON HAS A BEAUTIFUL FACE AND WILL LIVE WELL BECAUSE ONE JUST DOES WHAT ONE HAS TO DO WITHOUT DELUSIONAL THOUGHTS

Within their false mind worlds, people carry countless delusions, which are their false burdens, do false deeds, and then end up dying. The human mind worlds are made up of the pictures from the lives that they have lived that were taken and put into their brains, together with the habits and bodies. Every time the karma, habits, and bodies are discarded, people's faces brighten because the burdens in their minds disappear. When they become complete, people's faces become as bright and white as snow, and they are at their healthiest because their concerns, worries, and stress have disappeared.

A complete person is a person who has been born as Truth in the world of Truth. The body and mind of this universe are the Holy Spirit and Holy Soul. This body and mind can also be referred to as the Holy Father and Holy Mother. In Buddhism, that same existence is called the *Sambhogakaya* and *Dharmakaya*. When this existence of the universe body and mind, which is the world, comes as human beings, salvation can come to pass. The Holy Son will also come. When this existence comes as human beings, this existence will teach Truth and have people become Truth.

If people look for this existence in the outward appearance, this existence will not come, even if they wait for eternity. One can find that existence when they find Truth. If one eliminates one's sin, this existence of Truth will appear. At this time, we can find God, which is Truth.

Even the Nobel Peace Prize winner, Saint Teresa of Calcutta, expressed her mournful story of having neither seen nor met God. When one becomes free from one's sins, God can be found and seen. Now is the era to see and know God. Now is also the time to become this existence of Truth itself, be born again, and live eternally without death.

COMPLETE PERSON

In Korea, there are prophetic books called *JungGamRok* and *Gyeogam Yurok*, and these books say that 12,000 complete people will emerge.

There are numerous places in the world where people are cleansing their minds to achieve *Dō* (The Way, The Truth) in Buddhism or Taoism. They are all devoted to reaching *Dō*, but it will be impossible to achieve it without the method. Then what is *Dō*? *Dō* is the emptiness that is the source of this universe and Truth. Christians call this existence God; it can also be called Buddha, Allah, or *Haneolnim*. Although each religion refers to it differently, they are all talking about the existence of Truth.

Just as humans only speak, behave, and live according to what they possess in their minds, they cannot know God, Buddha, Allah, Truth, or *Dō* because they do not have it within them. For this existence to exist in a person's mind, one's karma, habits, and body must completely die. Then, there is *Dō* within your mind. So your mind has become one with Truth. When the place of *Dō* itself, which is Truth, becomes your mind and you are then reborn from there, you are a person who is born as Truth.

Just as people came into the world from a place of complete nothingness, when people leave this world after living in it, they will return to the place where there is nothing. Only when a person is born again from that place can they be reborn, resurrected, and live. Only the masters of the world, who are the Original Foundation, can make people be reborn as the masters of the world.

In Christianity, it is said that only 144,000 people will be saved. However, this number does not signify that exact number—instead, it means that many people will be saved. Similarly, the words referencing the 12,000 complete people do not mean that only 12,000 people will become complete; it means many people will become so.

In order to become one with Truth, one must eliminate one's karma, habits, and body, return to the Original Foundation, and be born from there.

Now is the time to become the Holy Son, saint, Buddha, and a Divine Being. If one's self, which is the karma, habits, and body, does not exist in the world, one arrives at the place of *Dō*, and when reborn from the Original Foundation, one is a complete person. Now is the time to become the Holy Son, saint, Buddha and a Divine Being. If one's self, which is the karma, habits, and body, does not exist in the world, one arrives at the place of *Dō* and when reborn from the original foundation, one is a complete person.

IN THE BUDDHIST SUTRAS

The *Mahayana Mahaparinirvana Sutra*, a Buddhist holy writing, said that the *mahayana mahaparinirvana* ("Big" death) and *parinirvana* (death without residue) can be achieved through *Dō* (The Way, The Truth) of the future. *Mahayana mahaparinirvana* refers to the great death where a person has completely disappeared. It means for one's karma, habits, and body to entirely disappear and for one to reach Truth. *Parinirvana* refers to dying the death without residue.

In the *Mahayana Mahaparinirvana*, it says that during the era of *Shakyamuni Buddha*, of the four virtues of *nirvana*: *nitya* (eternal permanence), *sukha* (bliss), *atman* (true self), and *suddha* (purity), only eternal permanence and purity can be enlightened. But in the latter days, all four virtues of *nirvana* will be enlightened. Previously, people could only see and know the eternal permanence and purity. It says in the days to come, people can also enlighten the true self and bliss when born again and thereafter live in Paradise.

When the masters of the Original Foundation come as human beings, they will enable people to be enlightened to the true self and bliss, and have people be born into and live in Paradise.

THE MEANING OF "RECEIVING THE SEAL"

It means to be marked with a seal. It is said that only people who have been marked with the seal shall live. This means that only the one who is reborn through the words of the world's masters can live; one has to be reborn along with the world from the mind of a person who has become the world. The world and the self will be born anew in the mind of the world that is Truth. They are born again by the words of the world's masters. This is what it means to receive the seal because the world and the self are born again within one's mind that has become Truth.

PART 3

PHILOSOPHY FOR A RIGHTEOUS CIVILIZATION

The fundamental answers to questions about life, existence, the mind and the world for a contemporary society.

WHAT IS PHILOSOPHY?

Philosophy is defined in the dictionary as the study of researching the fundamental principles of humankind and the world and topics such as the nature of life. In philosophy, people endeavor to find the origin of the world in their thoughts. However, no matter how much they try to find it, it cannot be found. This is because the world of Truth, which is the original essence, does not exist inside people's minds. This is why it cannot be found.

Philosophy and the Eastern word *Dō* (The Way, the Truth) are one and the same. But since the original essence of neither Philosophy nor *Dō* exists inside the human mind, they cannot be found. For these to exist inside the human mind, people, who are false, must disappear from the world. Then, the original essence, which is the true world, will exist inside the human mind. One can know all of these principles, including such things as the original essence of true life, and one will be able to take action.

WHO AM I?

Everyone has countless questions regarding this matter. Humans are not born into and living in the complete world, but rather are living inside their own mind worlds, which overlap the world. This is why humans are incomplete. In order to change these incomplete, false beings and make them become real and complete beings, the world of incompletion must be demolished, and they must be resurrected in the real world. This is how one can become a real person and live in the eternal Heaven and Paradise where there is no death.

A person who is born in eternal Heaven and Paradise is the master of the true world and a king. Just like Jesus, who was resurrected and came out of the stone tomb three days after his death, the one who has been resurrected and raptured is the master. When one has the true world inside one's mind, this person is the master of Heaven, humans, and earth.

WHAT IS THE FALSE SELF?

All people who are born in this world are the false and incomplete self. Humans are false because they live inside their illusions. These illusions consist of pictures of the universe that is Truth and their entire lives lived, which are stored in their mind worlds. People mistakenly believe that they are living in the world, but they have never lived in the world. Within the false worlds, they carry out false work and simply die—this is a person's life.

Inside their minds, which are false, people are slaves to the illusions because they live controlled by the false minds. Humans are slaves of those illusions because they live inside their false minds and live according to what their false minds direct them. The human mind is the karma, habit, and body, which are false. Every deed that is done while they have this human mind is not real. The self, which is a picture, is also not real. What is not real does not exist. One lives inside the world of his own videotape.

WHAT IS THE TRUE SELF?

People believe that they are born into and are living in this world, but they are incomplete because they live inside their own mind worlds, which are copies of the world. The human mind, which is false, is the karma, habit, and body. In order for people to become true, they have to discard the karma, habits, and body, make this universe that is Truth become their minds, and be reborn by the masters of Truth. The world and the people have to be born again from the universe mind that is Truth and become Truth to enable them to become their true selves. The world that is reborn as Truth after the falseness completely dies is Heaven and Paradise, which is the Land of Completion. This is a living world where, eternally, there is no death; it is great liberation and freedom. Here, one is the divine existence that has no concerns, worries, or stress. One is the child of God, Buddha, Allah, which is the existence of complete Truth. When one is reborn as Truth in the world where only Truth exists, he is Truth.

HOW DO YOU KNOW IF SOMETHING IS REAL OR FAKE?

What is real is Truth, and what is fake is false. The existence of God, Buddha, Allah is also real if it is Truth and fake if it is not Truth. The one who has Truth within his mind—one who has God, Buddha, Allah within his mind—is the one who believes in the real God, Buddha, Allah. The one who does not have this within him believes in a God, Buddha, Allah that is completely not real. Heaven, the Land of Bliss, Paradise are real for one who has God, Buddha, Allah within him; and for the ones who do not have it, it is all fake and, therefore, does not exist. It is the same for Truth. A person who has Truth inside his mind knows both what is true and what is false, and for one who does not, he knows neither what is true nor what is false. Only the one who has what is real within his mind can know.

WHO DO YOU THINK IS THE MOST SUCCESSFUL PERSON?

The idea of success depends on the standards in one's thoughts. Some may think money or power is what makes one successful; it all depends upon the person's consciousness. From the perspective of a person who has become Truth, there would be no way of life more valuable than becoming Truth and living forever. And there would be no other way of life more valuable than having people become Truth to live eternally. A person whose mind has become Truth will live that way.

HOW CAN WE PROGRESS TOWARDS A MORE TRUTHFUL WORLD?

Humans are incomplete because they do not live in the world but live inside the worlds of their minds, which overlap the world. They live mistakenly believing that they are living in the world. Since humans are living in nonexistent, illusionary worlds, they think false thoughts, do false deeds and end up dying in false worlds. A person's karma, habits, and body are false. When a person discards this falseness, one can be born in and live in the world of Truth, which is a truthful world. This is the path to human completion and the completion of the universe. Once a person becomes his complete self after discarding the self who is incomplete, he can be born in and live in the world of Truth, which is a good world.

AFTER DEATH, WILL OUR LIVES BE THE SAME AS OUR LIVES NOW?

The false self of a person is the karma, habits, and body. When this false self completely dies, one becomes the mind of *Jung* (Spirit) and *Shin* (Soul) of the universe emptiness, which is Truth and real. When one is then reborn from that land, this world and the self are reborn within his mind, so he will be living in the Land of Truth while still living in this world, and life and death will be one. One will be without worries, concerns, or stress and will live a life of freedom and liberation without suffering and burden in this land, right here. There is only the mind of happiness in the world of Truth where everything is alive.

WHAT WOULD BE THE MOST VALUABLE THING FOR HUMANKIND?

For people who live in the world, the most valuable thing is to live forever. There is nothing more valuable than this. The life that one lives after having become complete will be a good one because one does not have pain or stress, and it will be a life of freedom. This world and the afterworld are not two different worlds. The path of saving the people of the world will be the most valuable way of life.

WHO GOVERNS THIS WORLD?

When people ask who governs the world, they are asking who governs the life of people. All people think that after being born into this world, they are living by their own will. However, people live according to the movement of the celestial bodies of this universe and the position of the earth's movements, as do all creations. Because things in the world move and live according to the conditions of this world, there is an era of incompletion. Even the era of completion comes according to the movement of celestial bodies.

There must come a time when this world becomes complete and lives eternally, and also there must come a time when the world and people are reborn as Truth and live within the world of people's minds. The ultimate flow of everything is meant to transpire this way because all creations are the Spirit and Soul of the universe, and this existence that are the masters of the world created all creations in this world.

WHAT KIND OF PLACE IS HELL, WHERE IS IT, AND WHAT SHOULD I DO TO NOT GO THERE?

In Christianity, Buddhism, and Islam, they say that a person who has faith in Truth or faith in God, Buddha, Allah will go to Heaven, the Land of Bliss, Paradise, and a person who does not have faith will go to hell. They also say that those who do good deeds will go to Heaven, and those who do bad deeds will go to hell. We think that there are those who have gone to Heaven, the Land of Bliss and Paradise, which we have only heard of; but, the reality is completely different. The false self cannot exist in Heaven. There is no one who can go to Heaven without his mind having become Truth and having been born again as Truth in that Kingdom of Truth.

Heaven, the Land of Bliss, Paradise is when one's mind becomes Truth and lives eternally because one has the Land of Truth within one's mind. Heaven is the world that is born again from the sky (the Origin), and hell is the illusionary world people have been living in, which is the human mind world. When people die, they end up dying inside of that mind. They end up dying forever—imprisoned on earth, an eternal hell of ceaseless suffering. This is hell. People commonly think that they get burned in a fire and live with agony and burden in hell, but when they die in the false mind worlds, they just disappear. The way to escape from this is to discard the karma, habits, and body that are one's sins, and for the person who is false to become Truth.

HOW CAN YOU CHANGE YOUR LIFE?

People live in this world according to their minds. They speak and live according to as much as they have in their minds. The mind is formed by the habits that one is born with at birth, along with the karma formed during one's life lived. The unchangeable human mind world is one's selfish, narrow mind. One needs to completely destroy his false mind world in order to change to the mind of the living God of this great universe. Thereafter, you can live an improved life because you will know the principles of the world and have wisdom. You can live a complete life since your mind has changed. This is how to change your life to make it become complete.

WHAT ONE NEEDS TO DO IN LIFE

One lives in this world according to the inherited habits in the body with which he was born, and one's life lived—this is his mind world. The existence of the self lives having become a slave to this nonexistent mind. In a false world, one dreams false dreams, does false deeds, and then ends up dying. This is how people live.

People live in the nonexistent worlds as their nonexistent selves, which makes them not real but false. However, it is only when they become Truth that they will know this. For a long time, people have been living in the tunnel of the incomplete era. However, now the time has come for the era of completion.

At this time, people who have been incomplete until now must find their true selves by discarding their incomplete selves. Becoming real and true is everything in life. One should go from being his false self to becoming his true self. Rather than living in the nonexistent world, one should accumulate his blessings in the existent world. People should live without life or death in the eternally living world, together as one. This is what one should do with his life.

WHAT IS THE REASON AND PURPOSE WHY PEOPLE ARE BORN INTO THIS WORLD?

The Original Foundation of this universe is the emptiness. The celestial bodies such as the sun, the moon, and the countless stars in the sky came forth from this emptiness. The earth, which is also a star, then appeared. People and all creations came forth through the harmony of the sky and the earth. Every living thing in this world, and people, live according to the surrounding environment. People also live according to the environment of the sky and the earth. People have been living as incomplete beings for a long time in the environment created by the celestial bodies and the earth. But now is the time when anyone can achieve human completion and live. When the universe emptiness was the owner, people came from and went back to nothingness, which is the emptiness. For humankind to be saved, the masters of the emptiness have to come as human beings.

The reason and purpose why people came to this world is for people who are false to become true people. It is time for falseness to become Truth, achieve human completion, and live forever without death. The reason why people are born into the world is to become complete in the time of completion. For one's self to become complete, be born in the new world, and to exist without death is the reason and purpose one was born into this world. All material forms can only live up to their life spans, and then they disappear. However, everything in the world that is born inside the human mind is Truth, and everything lives forever. Isn't this the dream? When one goes to Heaven and Paradise, which is the Land of Truth, while living, one does not have death. One lives forever in this land, right here.

PART 4

THE ULTIMATE ASPIRATION OF RELIGION: TRUTH

The era for simply talking and searching for Truth has passed. Now is the time to find and confirm Truth.

WHAT IS RELIGION?

Originally, religion was about following the teachings of Truth. However, religious authorities are leading people to follow the interpretations of their minds instead of following Truth. Not only are people not becoming Truth, but they also do not know what Truth is or what the true will of Truth is. Now is the time to become Truth, know the true meaning of religion, and have Truth within and know it all.

WHAT IS THE PURPOSE OF RELIGION?

The ultimate purpose of religion is for a person's mind to go to Truth and be born in Heaven and Paradise, which is the Land of Truth. Although religions have been unable to fulfill this purpose, the time has now come in this universe when it can be realized. Now it is time to go to the eternally living Heaven and Paradise, the Land of Truth while living and become Truth, which is the true purpose of religion. It is time for one to repent, for one's mind to become the *Jung* (Spirit) and *Shin* (Soul) of the universe, and for the world and one's self to be born in that land.

WHAT IS THE ORIGIN OF RELIGION?

The origin of religion is the existence of the Original Foundation, which is the place where all creations in this world came from. Religion is where people discuss and speak of this existence. This existence is the existence of the Spirit and Soul, the body and mind of the universe, which is the true existence. This existence is the existence of the Holy Father and the Holy Spirit in Christianity, the existence of *Dharmakaya* and *Sambhogakaya* in Buddhism, and *Jung* (Spirit) and *Shin* (Soul) in the Korean folk religion that follows *Haneolnim*. People merely talked about this existence and did not have this existence within their minds, so there is only an abstract and conceptual God, Buddha, Allah, *Haneolnim*. Such an existence is an illusionary existence, so even if a person looks for all eternity, he can never know the existence of Truth that is God, Buddha, Allah, *Haneolnim*. Just as one can only know something when he has it within his mind, only the one who has God, Buddha, Allah, *Haneolnim*, and also the true world within him will have it. The origin of religion is Truth, and Truth is God, Buddha, Allah, *Haneolnim*. Now, you can only know the origin of religion when this existence exists within you.

WHICH RELIGION IS THE BEST RELIGION AND WHY?

The true religion among the religions would be the one that enables incomplete humans to become complete. Although there are countless religions in this world, none of them were able to make people become Truth. In Christianity, people believe in Jesus who came 2,000 years ago. In Buddhism, they believe in Buddha who came 2,500 years ago. In Confucianism, they believe in the teachings of Confucius. And then there are Hinduism, Islam, and tens of thousands of kinds of religions.

However, the true meaning of Christianity is the belief that Jesus will come again to save humankind, and in Buddhism, it also says that *Maitreya* will come to the world to save the people, and in *Seondo*, it says the *Jungdoryung*, the righteous leader of Truth, will come. There are so many different religions and their denominations, and each says that they have the true God. People do not have wisdom, and therefore, no one knows which one is the correct one. In order to properly know this, one has to seek God, Buddha, Allah, *Haneolnim* from within one's self to find it.

In the Bible, the Buddhist sutras, and the Qur'an, they also say that God, Buddha, and Allah, respectively, exists within the self and that one should not believe that it exists here or there. Each religion has given a name to this existence, but they all refer to the same existence of Truth. The ultimate purpose of religion is for this world and people to become complete and live eternally in the Land of Truth. Only the one who is born in Heaven and Paradise, the one who is born in the Land of Truth, while living, will be born into Heaven and Paradise "within you" and live there. When God, Buddha, Allah, *Haneolnim* that are Truth exist within one's mind, one should be born in that world to live eternally. This is how one can tell whether a certain religion is correct or not. The best religion is the place where one discards his karma, habits, and body that are one's sins, goes back to the original source, which is Truth, and is born again in that land.

DO WE NEED RELIGION?

Many people living in this world try to seek and gain something from outside of themselves, religion as well. However, once one escapes from his human mind world that is false, God, Buddha, Allah, *Haneolnim* that are Truth exist within. If this mind itself becomes that existence of Truth and is born again in the Land of Truth, which is this world, right here, it is the world of Truth. One can be reborn in this land, right here, and can live eternally by becoming created as the *Jung* (Spirit) and *Shin* (Soul). This is the rapture, the resurrection, having received the seal, and salvation. One should eliminate the mind of falseness within oneself, and find the place where Truth and the Land of Truth exist within oneself.

WHY ARE THERE SO MANY RELIGIONS?

All religions talk about the existence of Truth, which is the one and only Truth. However, people have their own interpretations, thus there are many denominations and religions. In the U.S., there are numerous denominations within Christianity alone. So if you are to ask which is the right place, you will find that the real place is the place where you can become the real Truth and go to the true world.

THERE IS ONLY ONE GOD IN THIS WORLD, BUT WHY ARE THERE SO MANY DIFFERENT RELIGIONS?

In this world, there is the existence of God that is Truth. It is the Spirit and Soul of the universe that are the *Jung* (Spirit) and *Shin* (Soul). This existence is the body and mind of the universe, which is the creator of all creations. In each place of religion, names were given to this existence, which is Truth. In Christianity, it is called God, in Buddhism it is called Buddha, and in Islam it is called Allah. The people who interpreted the Bible did so without having become Truth, which led to the formation of different denominations. Numerous denominations exist due to the interpretations, which came from the flawed human mind.

WHY DO PEOPLE BELIEVE IN RELIGION?

Each person believes in religion for different reasons—because one wants something with which to fill his mind, or he wants to go to a good place when he dies. Each person has a different number of reasons. However, it does not matter whether one believes in religion or not. What is important is that one becomes the Truth that is real and goes to the land of completion, which is the true world.

WHAT IS THE DIFFERENCE BETWEEN A RELIGION AND A CULT?

The ultimate purpose of religion is to become Truth and be born in the true world and live. There has been no method to become Truth in this world, and there was no one who could bring forth new birth in the true world. There has to come a time someday when people are made to become Truth and are brought to the true world.

Although there are numerous religions in this world, wouldn't they all be false if you cannot become the real Truth or go to the Land of Truth?

WHAT DO ALL RELIGIONS HAVE IN COMMON?

What religions have in common is that they teach that when the true existence comes to this world, people will go to the true world and be born as Truth. The scriptures are the book of prophecies that prophesied it. Now is the time for the self to cleanse one's mind, which is false, find Truth from within one's mind and go to the true world. Repenting, being absolved of one's sins, destroying one's false mind world, becoming Truth, and being born in the true world is the completion of this world.

DOES RELIGION UNITE US OR SEPARATE US?

Each place of religion has given the existence of Truth a different name—God, Buddha, Allah and *Haneolnim*. However, people who do not know the real meaning of Truth think that Christianity, Islam, Buddhism, and Hinduism are all different from each other. Because each thinks that one's own religion is correct, there is continuous fighting. If these are discarded and when all become the one Truth, everyone will become one. Religion cannot unite because Truth is called by different names and each particular religion believes itself to be right, making it impossible to unite. Now is the era when people can eliminate their false minds and become Truth. When people become Truth, they will go to the true world and everyone will become one while living.

WHY ARE THERE SO MANY DENOMINATIONS IN CHRISTIANITY?

Christianity is split into different denominations based on the differences in how people translated the words in the Bible. Denominations also formed due to self-centered interpretations and self-centered, greedy thoughts. People speak, live, and know only to the extent of what they have in their minds. People have no Truth within their different minds, and therefore their thoughts are also different, which gave rise to the numerous denominations. When people go to the place before they were born into this world and their minds become Truth, they will become the mind of oneness and there will be no denominations. Everyone should discard one's mistaken false mind, become the true mind, and be reborn.

DOES GOD EXIST?

The existence of God is the *Jung* (Spirit) and *Shin* (Soul), the universe emptiness of the non-material, actual existence that is omnipresent in this universe. This existence existed even before the beginning and this eternally existing existence of Truth is God, Buddha, Allah, *Haneolnim*. This existence is the creator of all material forms. Truth is a living existence, which existed before the beginning and will exist even after eternity. Only when the existence of the *Jung* and *Shin* of the universe come in human form, can the world be saved. The words of this existence are life. Truth that has come as human beings create the world. These existences eliminate the human mind that is incomplete so that only the true mind of the *Jung* and *Shin* of the universe remains, and create the new world and people from there. Only the masters of the world who have come as human beings can make the world be reborn within the human mind. Everything is then saved and this world can exist forever. These existences save everything in existence and nonexistence in this world.

WHY HAS GOD CREATED US?

When God created humankind and this world, it happened naturally and on its own accord. In Christianity, it is said that God created this entire world, and in Buddhism it is said that things were created according to the conditions of the earth, water, fire and wind. In Korea, it is said that things were born through the harmony of heaven and earth, which is nature, according to the circumstances. It seems like different things are being said, but they all mean the same thing. There must be a time when material entities and humans in the incomplete world can become complete. The *Jung* (Spirit) and *Shin* (Soul) of the universe, which exist without shape and form, created all material forms. The salvation that allows all to live in the complete universe can only be done when the *Jung* and *Shin* of the universe come as human beings who will save the entire world within the mind of a person who has become Truth.

IS IT POSSIBLE TO PROVE THE EXISTENCE OF GOD? OR IS IT IMPOSSIBLE?

The existence of God is the Spirit and Soul that is this infinite universe emptiness. The reason why people cannot see or know this existence is because it does not exist in their minds. A clergyman said that although there are many churches in this world, there is no one who has seen God or Heaven. God is not in a certain place somewhere. God is said to be within one's mind because it is an existence that can be seen when he discards his entire false human mind and has Truth in his mind. It is only possible to see God when one's self completely disappears from this universe. Thus, the existence of God can be proven. One can see and know this existence when the person, who is false, does not exist and when the *Jung* (Spirit) and *Shin* (Soul) of the universe have become one's mind.

WHERE IS GOD?

God is the non-material, omnipresent existence that exists everywhere in this world.

HOW CAN I FIND GOD?

God is the Spirit and Soul that is the universe emptiness, which is a non-material yet real and omnipresent existence. Humans do not know this because they do not have the *Jung* (Spirit) and *Shin* (Soul) of the universe within their minds. The *Jung* and *Shin*, which is the mind of the universe, only exist and are within one's mind when the human karma, habits, and body do not exist. This existence can only be found when it exists within one's mind.

WHAT DOES GOD MEAN?

God is the *Jung* (Spirit) and *Shin* (Soul) that is this universe emptiness. This existence is the creator of all material forms. Only when this existence comes as human beings can the creation of the Holy Spirit and Holy Soul be carried out and the whole world can be saved. This existence can only be found from within people's minds. God's purpose is to save—it is salvation.

HOW CAN I MEET GOD?

The way to meet God: this can be achieved when one's karma, habits, and body entirely cease to exist. God can be met in the place of nothingness, the place that existed before one was born, the place of the *Jung* (Spirit) and *Shin* (Soul) that is the universe emptiness. It is possible to meet God when one's self does not exist. When a person's mind has become Truth, one can see and know the *Jung* and *Shin* of the universe emptiness that has come to this world in human form. Only the one who does not have one's body and mind can meet God.

HOW CAN I FEEL THE EXISTENCE OF GOD?

As one discards one's false mind, God appears from within one's mind to the degree that the false mind is discarded. To that extent, realization will come—this is enlightenment. And when one becomes the existence of Truth, one will know all the ways of the world and will not have any unresolved questions or doubts because one becomes wisdom itself. When one goes to God's Kingdom and lives, it is happiness, freedom, and liberation because everything is alive. The ultimate purpose of humankind is to go to the living Kingdom of Truth, which never dies, and to live there.

WHY DO I NEED TO BELIEVE IN GOD?

God is the source of this world, the true existence and the *Jung* (Spirit) and *Shin* (Soul), which is the emptiness and the Origin. Unless this existence becomes a person's mind, the self and the world cannot be reborn from within one's mind. To believe in God means to become one with God. To become one, all people must repent their sins and make their minds become the *Jung* and *Shin*, which is the universe mind. When the false self completely disappears and only Truth remains, God, which is Truth, exists within one's mind because God is Truth. Until now, completion was not possible because this time in the world had not yet come. Hereafter, if a person is absolved of his sins and his mind is reborn in this land, he can live eternally. This is possible when the world and people become Truth and are reborn in this land. Now, it is possible to become complete.

PART 5

ANY QUESTIONS? ASK ME.

Just as computers in this twenty-first century are enhanced with artificial intelligence, in this new era, people should enhance themselves with True Wisdom. With True Wisdom, you can know the answers to all. This section covers solutions and resolutions to YouTube's most sought out questions about life.

I. THE MIND

WHAT IS THE MIND?

The human mind is the accumulation of one's life lived based on the habits; that is one's mind. When you throw this away and become the universe mind, this is the true mind. The human mind is the pictures that one has taken of the things in the world throughout one's life. What exists inside one's mind are false and pictures. Since those pictures are not real, humans are incomplete. If one discards this false mind, becomes the mind of the world that is Truth, and is born again, then this is the mind of Truth that is real and alive.

WHAT CAN I DO TO CLEANSE MY MIND? HOW CAN I CLEANSE MY MIND?

What does it mean to have a clean mind? When one discards the human mind and becomes the mind of the great universe, one has cleansed his mind and made it clean.

The mind of emptiness, which is the mind of the universe, is a mind that has absolutely nothing. It is the mind in which everything has completely ceased. A person has thoughts arising to the degree he possesses his own mind. But one who does not have his own mind does not have these thoughts, and his mind is clean because he does not have this mind. When one completely discards everything one remembers, the habits, and the body, one's mind will become clean.

HOW TO ELIMINATE STRESS

People get stressed when they struggle with what they are doing, when things do not work out as they expected, and when there is no progress as a result. And when other incidents happen in addition to all of that, considerable stress adds up. All of this stress comes from the self-constructed and narrow mind that is unable to accept. For example, even when people face the same issue, some will experience less stress and others more. The level of stress experienced depends on the size of the individual's mind.

People's stress exists in their own minds and is triggered when their minds cannot accept something. Whereas, when you discard this, and have the mind that has absolutely nothing in it, you will have no stress. When you discard and eliminate the karma and habits that are within you, there is no stress.

ANXIETY RELIEF: HOW TO DEAL WITH ANXIETY

Anxiety means one becomes anxious when one cannot handle his or her mind.

Some people do not get anxious even under uneasy circumstances, but others get anxious because their minds lack inner strength.

In one's mind, there is a lot of anxiety if one has lived an anxious life in the past. When you throw away the life lived and the circumstances in your life that have caused anxiety, the anxiety disappears.

To become complete, discard your karma, habits, and body; discard your human mind, change to the mind of the world, and be born again in the world. Then, there is no anxiety.

HOW TO ELIMINATE WORRIES

Every person has worries. Worrying is being concerned about future events before they even happen. One has worries when one has no confidence in his mind.

One has worries when he cannot do his job properly. One has worries when he is not satisfied with the realities of the life he is living.

In order to eliminate these worries, discard your mind that gives rise to the worries; then, there will be no worries.

HOW TO BE FREE FROM THOUGHTS: HOW TO STOP OBSESSIVE THOUGHTS

Human thoughts come from one's own mind.
In the mind, there is the body that one has inherited from parents, habits, and one's life lived. This is one's mind. Thoughts arise from this mind.

In order to be free from thoughts, throw away the mind, the root of the thoughts. Then, thoughts will disappear.

INNER PEACE

While everyone seeks inner peace, there is no one who is truly at peace. For the world to be harmonious and people to have inner peace, people's minds have to become true.

However, in the mind that one has built up over one's lifetime, there is only stress and, therefore, there is no inner peace.

When you discard this mind of stress, you will have a peaceful mind, which is the mind of Truth. So why not try this meditation of throwing away the body and mind?

HOW TO CONTROL AND MASTER YOUR EMOTIONS

Human emotions come from the minds one has. Emotions exist in the mind, habits, and body that one came to have while living. Once you discard these and reach the true mind, which is the mind of Truth, there are no such thing as emotions. There is only the mind that accepts everything. This is falseness becoming Truth.

HOW TO OVERCOME GUILT AND REGRET

Many people have regrets about their lives. Only after time passes do people come to have regrets—thinking that their lives could have been better. People also regret the mistakes they made in relationships with others and the wrongdoings of the past. Such regret is no different than a meaningless dream that has already passed.

You can get rid of these regrets from your mind by eliminating the cause of these regrets, which are the related events. When you get rid of all the remembered thoughts of the life you lived, you will have no more regrets.

HOW NOT TO BE ANGRY

Anger is an emotion that arises when people encounter something that does not suit their tastes. Anger differs from person to person, but it arises when one faces one's weaknesses or a situation that one does not like.

When one eliminates one's life lived, which is the source of anger, and also discards the habits, anger does not exist. A person has anger because one has that mind.

WHAT DOES IT MEAN TO HAVE COMPLETE FREEDOM THROUGH AWAKENING?

Awakening comes when you discard and break free from your fixed conceptions, customs, and habits. The more you break away from them, the more you realize—this is what awakening is.

The human mind is an illusion, which is not real. As much as that falseness disappears, Truth enters your mind. And at that time, when you realize it, your mind will enlighten, "Aha!" To put it simply, when the falseness is broken down, you become Truth. When you become Truth, you will enlighten as much as you have become Truth. Awakening to everything and absolute freedom is when none of your mind exists. Then, you become the mind of the great universe, and when you are born again from there, you can be enlightened to it all and have great freedom.

HOW TO BE HAPPY AND POSITIVE ALL THE TIME

People think happiness is when they have what others envy. People think they will be happy if they make lots of money, have a beautiful woman by their side, have a child who does well at school, or when their goals are achieved. But at the end of this happiness, there is inevitable loss, and that is when people become miserable.

True happiness is when people's minds do not have the mind to pursue happiness. When one has escaped from the human mind, which is filled with greed, then one will always be happy. The mind of Truth that is always alive, the mind of nothingness, is the mind that accepts anything that comes its way. So, it is happiness itself.

As long as the self exists, there is no happiness in one's desires. When one's self, which is false and not real, disappears, one becomes the true self and is always happy.

GRATITUDE

People do not know to be grateful for being born into and living in this world because they live inside their own minds. Since people live according to the greed in their minds, they live continuously complaining. People's blessings are founded in a grateful and generous mind, as people with that mind find that everything works out smoothly and so they can succeed.

When one is grateful for every single thing in his life, he will live a truly happy life. Though they try, people cannot be grateful because their minds are negative, and they do not have gratitude within. People can only have gratitude when they change their negative minds to positive, grateful minds. When one casts off his negative mind, which is a false mind, only the grateful mind remains.

THE POWER OF MIND

People act and live based on what they have in their minds, and they live as slaves to that. The power of mind depends on how much confidence one has in his mind; the mind has as much power as there is confidence in his mind. In the minds that humans have, there is no confidence. Thus, the human mind changes all the time.

However, if you become the universe mind, which is Truth, rather than the constantly changing human mind, your mind will not fluctuate. Therefore, you will always just focus on what you do, and you will be able to achieve whatever you want to achieve with the power of mind.

WHAT IS DEPRESSION AND HOW TO GET RID OF IT?

Depression is when reality does not live up to one's desires and thoughts. This is when one develops depression. Such a phenomenon occurs because one overestimates himself, and his own assessment of himself does not coincide with reality. When one has an inflated image of himself, how he sees himself in his own fantasy is far from how he is in reality. Since there is such a wide gap between his fantasy and the reality of the world, he becomes frustrated, which in turn makes him become depressed.

Depression can be overcome when he discards his life lived, habits and body, and is reborn after having become one with the mind of the world where there is no mind of the self.

HOW TO BE COURAGEOUS AND BOLD

While living in this world, a courageous person endeavors to push ahead in his work with conviction. It is rare to find such a bold person because most people do not have the mind of courage. When you eliminate the countless minds in the human mind, then only the mind of courage, which is Truth, remains. This will allow you to be proactive and courageous in what you do.

The boldest and most courageous person is the one who fully applies himself to the task at hand since he has absolutely no human mind and has only the true mind. Discard the human mind that is not true but false. When you cleanse your mind to be born in the true mind, you will be a truly courageous person.

HOW TO DEAL WITH LONELINESS

Loneliness is an emotion people feel when they do not receive acknowledgment from others and when they are alone. They feel lonely when they cannot control their own minds and when their minds feel empty. They also feel lonely when none of the relationships they have are fulfilling. All of this comes from the unsatisfied desires in one's mind, and these disappear when one discards the falseness, which is one's mind. Loneliness disappears when one discards the entire life lived, the illusionary habits, and the body.

HOW TO MEDITATE PROPERLY: TRUE MEDITATION METHOD

People often meditate in various ways to attain enlightenment, know the ways of the world, and also become saints and enlightened beings.

Until now, there have been numerous different types of meditation: ones where you sit still, think about a certain topic and only focus on that, or intentionally put the body through discomfort, etc. However, no one has truly been enlightened. If a meditation method truly works, anyone who meditates according to the method should become enlightened.

There is no enlightenment for a person who lives in the human mind world, which is made by taking pictures and copying the things of the world. This is because there is no Truth in one's mind. Enlightenment comes when the true mind is revealed to the degree that the false mind has been eliminated.

In the Bible, it is stated that one should believe in one's heart and confess with one's mouth. When there is no falseness, only Truth remains and you will confess, "Ah, this is it!" When you do the meditation of eliminating the self, you will enlighten and become Truth. Thus, this is the true meditation method.

HOW TO LET GO

The habits and karma, which people have within their minds, do not disappear unless they are discarded. The way to let go is to eliminate the habits, karma, and body that are within one's mind.

For example, if you have hatred or an enemy in your mind, it disappears when you eliminate the karma, habits, and body, and all that is in your mind also gets discarded. When you eliminate the habits and karma, which are the human mind, you can become the true mind, which is Truth, and can be free and liberated without suffering or burden. You can be reborn in the Land of Truth and live forever.

WHAT IS THE PURPOSE OF LIFE?

People think the reason and purpose of living in this world is to accumulate wealth and to gain fame, but those are just a means to make a living. The true reason and purpose of life is to become a true person and to live a true life. One's mind must become Truth to live a true life, and one must be reborn in the Land of Truth. This is the reason why humans are born into the world. One came to this world to live eternally. To live eternally, one must attain human completion.

To reach human completion, one must eliminate his body and mind so that only Truth remains and then be reborn from Truth and live. This is the reason and purpose why one is born into the world.

Until now, there was no method to reach human completion and live eternally. The time for the existence of this method has now arrived.

WISDOM: HOW TO BE WISE

Wisdom does not exist in the human mind, which is fake. Wisdom exists when one becomes the universe mind itself, which is real. Wisdom comes from a clean mind, and one has as much wisdom as he has cleansed his mind.

One enlightens to the logic of things and comes to know when one has the universe mind that is wisdom. Things cannot be known when seen from the perspective of the human mind; things can only be known when seen from the universe's perspective. This is what wisdom is.

One who has the true mind has wisdom, and so one is able to resolve all things and take action according to nature's flow. One whose false self does not exist and has been reborn as the true self is a wise person.

II. PERSONAL DEVELOPMENT

BE IN THE MOMENT. HOW TO LIVE IN THE MOMENT

Everyone living in this world dreams false dreams, does false deeds, and then ends up dying. Because people are too busy regretting their past, worrying about the future, and being obsessed with things that do not actually exist, their lives are not grounded in reality.

If you want to be realistic, you should eliminate the life lived of the self, habits, and body. Your mind then becomes the living consciousness of the true world, which is the realistic mind. Your mind becomes the mind that can be dedicated to the work you do in the present. Consequently, you will be successful in what you do because you will do your utmost, which will make you a capable person.

People are unable to live in the present moment because of the countless thoughts within themselves. All of these thoughts are either about the past, which is nothing but a nonexistent mind, or about the future, which also does not exist. All of these countless thoughts are nonexistent.

When you discard these thoughts and become real and true, there is only this present moment. You will then be realistic and efficient in what you do, which will enable you to also live well in the future. If you work hard now and create results, you will reap tomorrow what you sow today.

HOW TO BREAK BAD HABITS

The habits that people have are the habits that they inherited from their ancestors at birth, combined with their lives lived; this is what habit is.

Unless you discard these habits, it is extremely difficult to change your habits, and they are not easily fixed. In order to change your habits, you should discard the habits, which are ingrained in the root of your mind. The habits can then be broken.

HOW TO FOCUS AND IMPROVE CONCENTRATION

People cannot concentrate well because they have countless minds embedded inside their minds. This is why people cannot concentrate on what they are doing. Concentration is when you can focus only on what you are doing at that moment.

To have good concentration, you should eliminate the countless wrongful minds, which allows only the true mind to remain. Then, you can concentrate well.

POSITIVE THINKING: HOW TO BE POSITIVE

For people to have positive minds, it is impossible to achieve it within their own minds. Because people have self-centered and biased minds, they have the minds of envy, jealousy, criticism, good, bad, existence, and nonexistence. Such things exist in their minds because their own minds exist.

When people get rid of their minds and become the true mind, then they will have a positive mind, which is an accepting mind. When people have a positive mind, they can always live a positive life. Since they are positive, the work that they do is positive, and so things in their lives will work out seamlessly.

For those who are negative, nothing suits their minds. Thus, what they do in the world is also not positive, and they cannot take action. This is why they cannot achieve.

If a person wants to live a positive life, one should change one's negative mind to the positive mind. The method to change the mind is to throw away the negative mind.

AS COMPUTERS ARE ENHANCED WITH ARTIFICIAL INTELLIGENCE, PEOPLE SHOULD BE ENHANCED WITH TRUE WISDOM

Just as computers in this twenty-first century are enhanced with artificial intelligence (AI), people should enhance themselves with True Wisdom. In Go matches between computers programmed with AI and professional human players, the Go pros lost to the computers equipped with AI. This twenty-first century is the era for people to have True Wisdom so that they can know everything. People should become saints and sages.

To solve and give the method to solve the questions on YouTube, people must become free from their fixed notions, habits, and customs and see things from the perspective of the universe, which is Truth. Everything will then be solved.

When one throws away one's false body and mind and finds one's true self, one will become a complete person. All matters concerning religion, philosophy, ideology, academics, and life will then be resolved.

This True Wisdom is what people living in the twenty-first century must obtain. A person with True Wisdom can solve, by oneself, all of mankind's unresolved questions and doubts as well one's personal unresolved questions and doubts.

BE GRATEFUL: THE SECRET TO HAPPINESS

To be happy means to become the true mind. The true mind is happiness itself.

It is the mind that accepts everything at all times and has absolutely no judgments that arise from human life. That is the thankful mind, which is happy.

One is grateful when one has a big mind. So eliminate the false mind, be born in the true world with the true mind, which is Truth. Then one will always be happy for there will only be the thankful mind.

HOW TO LIVE WELL

People think that they can measure and evaluate how good their lives are depending on whether they have a lot of money, have good food to eat, have nice clothes to wear, or have a fancy house to live in.

However, people who are living this way live with even more suffering and burden within their countless agonizing thoughts.

People can live good lives when they have no suffering or burden, have a peaceful mind, and are able to take pride in and just focus on the work that they do without useless thoughts. This way, they can live well without lacking materialistically or in any other aspects of life.

Those who have no stress—worries, suffering, and burden—and have the mind that accepts everything in the world, are the ones who live well.

One who has a positive mind, whose mind is Truth and is born and living in the true world, is the one who is living well and the one who is living a happy life.

When your false self does not exist, and you are born again as the true self while alive, you will live well.

SELF-DEVELOPMENT TIPS

Self-development is awakening the wisdom that is latent inside you. This can be achieved when you throw away what you have in your mind and become the mind that is alive. This is wisdom. Wisdom does not come from the false human mind; it comes when you become the mind of Truth.

To develop yourself, completely eliminate your body and mind—then you have wisdom. This is self-development.

HOW TO BECOME SMART AND WISE

To be smart means to be wise.
It is not possible to be wise when one's mind is only occupied with a self-centered mind. When you throw away your self-centered mind and have the true mind, your words and actions are righteous. When you are righteous, you will speak objectively, and you will become smart.

Being smart means that when you speak, your words are easily understood by others, and your words are communicated to others effectively.

When you discard your self-centered mind and have an objective mind, you can become smart.

HOW TO STAY MOTIVATED AND NOT GIVE UP

The reason why people have thoughts about wanting to give up while they are in the middle of doing something is that their minds are not determined enough.

At this time, if a person comes to have the true mind, which is life, in one's mind, the mind that wants to give up disappears, and one will not give up.

It is because there are too many illusions coming from one's countless false minds that people want to give up.

However, if you have the true mind, you can simply do what you do and only do that. This way, you have strength and courage, which will make you act with passion and you can get good results in what you do.

When you get rid of your negative mind and have a positive mind, you will not give up.

HOW TO HAVE CONFIDENCE

If you want to have confidence, you need to have confidence in the work that you do. This is when you have confidence. Confidence is when you have the capability to handle the work you are trying to do. Only then, you have confidence.

All of these things are the same—they are worries about the future. Worries regarding the future come from one's failures in the life one has lived. Depending on how much, or how little, sense of inferiority one possesses from those failures, one has a lot, or little, confidence. When you eliminate this sense of inferiority, you will become confident.

If you get rid of all the times when you were falling behind in life and your mind goes to the original mind, your mind of inferiority disappears, and you will have confidence.

HOW TO NOT BE BORED

If you do not want to be bored, you need to have something to do; then, you will not be bored. When you are bored, the most effective solution is to eliminate the cause of your boredom. Since what you have in your mind is what causes you to feel bored and lonely, if you remove the source of that mind, the boredom and loneliness will disappear. So practicing this meditation of eliminating your mind is the best remedy.

MEDITATION FOR IMPROVING CONCENTRATION

People cannot stay focused due to the countless thoughts they have come to have throughout their lives. If a person gets rid of these thoughts, they will disappear. If one discards the life one has lived and eliminates the illusions in the mind, one will not have this mind. You will only have the living mind of wisdom, and you will be able to stay focused and achieve the best results.

This is also true when you are studying or working. If you are to be acknowledged by others wherever you go, your mind should concentrate on only one thing—whether it be your studies or work. By doing so, you can create results, and then others will acknowledge you. To do this, one needs intensive meditation.

OVERCOMING PROCRASTINATION: HOW TO STOP BEING LAZY

The reason why people put things off is either that there is something that they have to do at the moment or out of habit. People tend to procrastinate when their minds are complicated. When you eliminate this complicated mind, you will naturally take action and not procrastinate. Once you eliminate the mind that stops you from moving your body and taking action, you will be able to take action without procrastinating.

PRODUCTIVITY HACK: HOW TO BE PRODUCTIVE

Wisdom and productivity come when a person is focused on the work that one does without any minds or distractions. You can be the most productive when you pour your heart into the work that you do and aim to be the absolute best.

Once you eliminate the mind that is distracted by many thoughts, you will be left with the mind that can simply focus on the task.

REAL SELF-DISCIPLINE: HOW TO BUILD SELF-DISCIPLINE AND MAKE IT POSSIBLE

Even the most inspiring quotes or sayings cannot be put into action if your mind is filled with falseness. Although people try to act according to these great words, they end up failing because the thought that they should do so only lasts for a moment. This is because there are countless minds within the self, which make self-discipline impossible.

The only way to have self-discipline is to change to the mind of Truth after discarding your own mind. You are then discipline itself. You are complete, and you are a complete person without any inadequacies. Therefore, one is discipline itself without even the mind of discipline. You become complete when you discard your mind, which is illusionary. This is the ultimate self-discipline.

KNOW YOUR REAL VALUE

As people live in this world, many people put value in making things happen according to their will. However, what is truly valuable is for a person to become the living Truth.

Without becoming the living Truth, there is no real value in a person's achievements as those achievements are all illusory.

What is truly valuable for humankind is for incomplete people to become complete and live together with all the people of this world.

A person's real value lies in becoming the living Truth and living forever; those who have produced many results in the Land of Truth have value.

The valuable ones are those who go from being in the incomplete, false world to being born and living in the true world, which is complete.

THE WAY TO IMPROVE YOUR LIFE

People live with suffering and burden because they live inside the mind worlds that they themselves have made, which are false worlds and worlds of sin.

As long as one holds onto this mind world, his life cannot improve because he lives speaking and acting solely according to the mind that he has. This way, a person cannot improve his life.

When a person eliminates one's mind, he will clearly know all the principles of the world, and his life will be completely different. One will be able to live a happy life where he can live well because he has wisdom and will put it into action.

HOW TO LOVE YOURSELF

Humans are incomplete and have lived their lives in a self-centered way; being only concerned with themselves. People live in a world where they are only concerned with their incomplete selves. Humans have such love and affection for the illusion that they cannot have it in their minds to try to understand and love that which belongs to others.

Despite their love for their false selves, they end up dying because they are false. They end up dying without their lives having had any meaning or significance.

In the Bible, it says that those who try to die will live, and those who try to live will die. This means that when your self, which is false, dies, you can go to Truth, be born as Truth, and live. Therefore, instead of keeping your false self, discard it, become true, and live eternally. Surely, this would be the way to truly love yourself? The only way to love yourself is to discard the self who is false and find your true self. Only those who repent are the ones who truly love themselves.

III. HEALTH & LONGEVITY

LONGEVITY SECRETS: HOW TO LIVE LONGER

If a person wants to live a long life, one must always have an accepting mind. Only then, will one be able to live long. One who has a negative mind is constantly stressed, so *qi* (energy) and blood cannot circulate well throughout the entire body. In this way, one cannot live a long life.

One who has thrown away all the self-centered minds and stress has a positive mind and therefore can live long. So one will naturally eat and exercise adequately because one has wisdom.

DEEP SLEEP SECRET: HOW TO SLEEP WELL

For a person to sleep well, one should move the body all day long.

Subsequently, once you eliminate all of the life lived recorded in your mind and become the true mind, you can sleep well. You need to sleep well to stay healthy, so you should be a person who moves diligently throughout the day.

You should also eliminate your mind, which is stress, and then you will be able to sleep deeply.

HOW TO NATURALLY BOOST YOUR IMMUNE SYSTEM

In order to boost their immune systems, people do many things such as adopting vegetarian diets, eating foods that enhance immunity, or taking medicine. However, because they do not stay consistent, they can sometimes get sick.

The best way to boost immunity is to ensure good circulation of *qi* (energy) and blood. In order to improve circulation, discard the mind, which is stress. Then, the circulation will improve throughout your entire body, and so will your immunity.

Since the body and mind are one, when you have a comfortable and peaceful mind, your body has the strongest immunity. The best way to boost your immunity is to get rid of the human mind, which is stress, and change to the mind of the world, which is the big mind.

MENTAL HEALTH TIPS: HOW TO IMPROVE MENTAL HEALTH

People have many physical and psychological illnesses because they have a lot of minds in their consciousness, which are their minds. One becomes ill when things do not happen as one desires.

If one throws away all the negative minds he has inside his mind, only the true mind remains. Then, illness will disappear.

When there is only the true mind, one can become healthy in body and mind. Illnesses come from the poor circulation of *qi* (energy) and blood in the body, so when one eliminates one's mind, *qi* and blood circulation will improve, leading to a healthy mind and body.

HOW TO HEAL YOUR ENTIRE BODY AND MIND

People are peculiar because their minds are unnatural—their bodies and minds are off balance. People are unnatural because they cannot become one with the righteous world, and they cannot live in the world because they live inside their minds.

To heal your body and mind, you should get rid of your false human mind world, be born again in the world, and live there. Then your body and mind will be completely healed.

THE BEST MEDITATION

The reason and purpose why people meditate: because humans are incomplete, they meditate to become complete. Completion means falseness becomes Truth. When falseness becomes Truth, there is no further meditation to be done.

There are numerous kinds of meditation practices: meditation where you contemplate one topic, stillness meditation, breathing meditation, and meditation where you focus your gaze on a candle flame. However, for a person to reach human completion and to achieve the purpose of meditation, it is not possible to achieve while one's mind still remains. Without discarding one's mind, one's body will only become fatigued from all the sitting.

If you subtract and eliminate all of your false mind, Truth will exist in your mind, and you will enlighten as much as there is Truth in your mind. Then, only the true mind remains. From there, if you are born again in the true world, Truth is within you and the Land of Truth is within you. You can achieve human completion and become a saint.

This meditation of discarding the false world and being born in the true world is the ultimate meditation. Once you achieve human completion, there is no further meditation to do.

LAUGHTER IS THE BEST MEDICINE

In Eastern culture, there is a saying that laughter brings good luck and there is also another saying that laughter is good for your health. People can laugh when they have a positive and big mind. While the mind is laughing, there is no mind of stress. Laughter is the best medicine among all medicines because it makes the *qi* (energy) and blood circulate well. People who can always laugh do not have the mind of stress so they are healthier, can live longer, and also live a better life than those who do not laugh.

HOW TO KEEP YOUR BRAIN HEALTHY

Every disease that people have stems from one's mind of stress that blocks the circulation of *qi* (energy) in the affected parts of the body. This is how diseases form. The brain improves and becomes healthier when one eliminates his mind of stress, which is the entirety of his remembered thoughts and the images of the brain.

HOW TO LOSE WEIGHT

People gain weight because they do not move after eating food; this way, all of the food becomes extra weight.

If people eat adequately, move a lot, and exercise, they will not gain weight. Instead of eating as much food as you want, eat an appropriate amount, and exercise a lot. Eating adequately is when you eat just short of being full, and it is best to just eat three times a day and not in between. It also is not good to binge-eat after skipping meals, or eat too much of what you enjoy.

People who have a lot of thoughts in their minds have difficulty controlling their eating habits. When people are stressed, they tend to eat a lot and gain a lot of weight. If people eliminate their minds, which is the source of their thoughts, they will eat about, or less than, a third of what they used to eat and will not gain unnecessary weight.

HOW TO QUIT SMOKING, DRUGS, AND ALCOHOL

It is very difficult for people to just quit smoking, drugs, and alcohol.

When a person eliminates all the anecdotes of smoking, drugs, and alcohol in his mind and his self, he returns to the Origin. When one is reborn from the Origin, the self who used to smoke, do drugs, and drink alcohol disappears. At that time, he quits when told, "The way to quit smoking, doing drugs, and drinking alcohol is to just stop doing it." I have seen this to be the case for many people. For those who cannot quit, they all quit when they are asked, "Are you going to let the cigarette, drugs, and alcohol get the best of you?"

HOW TO NATURALLY LOOK YOUNGER THAN YOUR AGE

To look younger, people often put on makeup, eat healthy foods or take medicine. However, when there is no suffering, stress, and burden in a person's mind, one's face relaxes and looks youthful.

People age and get wrinkles on their faces because they have suffering and burden. This happens because one's *qi* (energy) does not circulate well, and the cells in one's bodies cannot function properly.

We have observed countless cases of people who discard their stress, pain and burdens and appear younger. Not only do they appear much younger, but their faces also glow when there is no mind, and they become the most beautiful version of themselves.

Eliminating your mind is the method to look younger, and you will also be healthier than ever.

THE WAY TO HEAL YOURSELF

People live with countless agonies, suffering and burden because they have only been adding things to the world of their minds since they came to live in the world. Consequently, they now have so much in their minds. This is why there are mental illnesses and physical illnesses, which are also caused by those minds. Once those minds are discarded, it is often observed that people's physical and mental illnesses both improve.

Incomplete humans are incomplete because they live within their minds. When they discard those minds, their minds and bodies become true, and they become healthy. All illnesses exist in the mind.

Do the study of eliminating the self, which is false, and be reborn. Thereafter, when born and living in the true world, illnesses disappear.

The way to heal one's illnesses is for one's false mind to become true. I have witnessed changes in many people. Everything exists in the mind, so once the mind is eliminated, the stress that is tied to it disappears, and the body and mind become healthy.

IV. RELATIONSHIPS

HOW TO COMMUNICATE EFFECTIVELY WITH PEOPLE

Listen carefully to what others say and do not judge them as being right or wrong. Also, accept what others say with a positive mind. Do not insist on your own opinion, and speak true words so that people have confidence in you.

When you throw away your false mind and have the true mind, you can sincerely listen to what the other person has to say. Consequently, another person can trust, listen and be accepting of any offered opinions.

Since people have self-centered, selfish minds, they only talk from their own perspectives. However, such words cannot move the hearts of others.

Others will listen to your sincere words when your mind has become Truth.

One who has discarded his own false mind can make others trust him and can move their hearts.

HOW TO MAKE PEOPLE LIKE YOU

People like others with big minds who do not impose their will on others and are able to accept others. If you want to be liked, you need to have a big mind.

Always be humble and sincere; when you have these minds, others will like you.

Compliment others, then, they will like you. Your sincere mind remains when you eliminate your false mind. When you become that sincere mind, others will like you.

HOW TO GET ALONG BETTER WITH PEOPLE

To get along well with people, one should not have an ego or boast about oneself.

You can get along well with people and be liked when you are not opinionated and when you can sincerely accept what others say.

When you are able to accept different people regardless of how they are, then you can get along with others. It is easy to get along with others after eliminating the narrow mind and changing to the mind of the world. You just have to discard the self-centered mind.

HOW TO TREAT OTHERS

Treat others with ease so as to not burden them. Instead of forcing what you have to say on others, listen carefully to what they say and accept their opinions. Always treat others with the mind that has become Truth and without any expectations. Talk about their strengths, not about their weaknesses or wrongdoings. Embrace what others say and do. If you treat others with the big mind of Truth, which is absent of mind, they will always like you. Therefore, you should throw away your false mind and find the true mind.

HOW TO BE ATTRACTIVE TO EVERYONE

For a person to be attractive, one should only focus on what one does, work hard, and produce results. When one is broadminded and has a big heart, is at ease when working, is always positive, and is able to keep a smile on his face when working and interacting with others, one is attractive. A person who always has this mind and lives this way without change is attractive. However, one cannot force oneself to have this mind. One's mind naturally becomes this attractive mind when one eliminates his own mind, which is the life lived, habits, and body, and has the mind of the great universe, which is the Origin. Then, one becomes attractive.

WHAT IS LOVE? TRUE MEANING OF LOVE

Love. True love is acceptance without expecting anything in return. People often use the words, "I love you." But this is said to control others in order to fulfill one's greed. This is not true love.

In Christianity, it is said that only God's love is true love because God has only the mind of acceptance. Therefore, it is true love without any judgements or minds about what is good or bad. A person can love unconditionally only when the mind is discarded and the mind of the great universe is always present. Love is not to be received, but to be given. When true love is given, true love can be received. One must have the true mind to truly love.

RACIAL PREJUDICE AND DISCRIMINATION

Racial prejudice and discrimination are the behaviors of people who have only ever known their own perceptions and do not have the universal consciousness.

When people discard their self-centered minds and have the true mind of the great universe, they will enlighten that everyone is one. When they know this, there cannot be any racial prejudice and discrimination. When people realize that the concept of black, white, or yellow comes from one's perceptions and they change to the big, complete mind, they realize that everyone in this world is, in fact, one's own self. People of this world will then become one, and racial prejudice and discrimination will not be able to exist.

When a person discards one's mind, which is the lived life, habits, and body that are illusions, goes to the big mind and is born again, there is no longer any racial prejudice and discrimination, and everyone can live as one.

HOW TO MAKE FRIENDS

People usually make friends with those who have the same state of mind as their own. All people prefer people who have similar states of mind to their own, and they try to befriend those who can understand them and those who like them. Instead of trying to make a friend or expecting something from them, change your mind to have a genuine mind and be sincere when making friends. Being sincere is the way to find unwavering friendship. If your mind is truthful, others will treat you truthfully, truly understand, and become your friend. The way to find true friends is discarding your false mind and becoming the true mind—then, you can have true friends in life.

HOW TO BE IN HARMONY AND GET ALONG WITH OTHERS

Everyone in this world lives together with others while they live in this world, but there are many who are living selfish lives that are far too self-centered. To be in harmony with others, one needs to have a big mind. It is difficult because the self-centered mind only wants to live according to its own narrow-minded thoughts and, therefore, cannot be in harmony with others within a group.

When one eliminates one's life lived and habits, becomes the mind of the world, and lives life, his life will not be difficult because he can accept everything.

When one lives the life of nature's flow, he will not have conflicts or hang-ups and, thus, will be able to be in harmony with others within a group. He will be able to get along well with others because others will like him.

Therefore, one can become successful because he will not have conflicts with others, and others will approve of him. The most important thing in life is to discard one's narrow, false mind, become the true mind, which is the big mind, and live. This way, one can be in harmony and achieve everything he wishes to achieve.

HOW TO BE A GOOD PARENT

If you are to be a good parent, you need to become a true person. This way, your children will be emotionally stable because you will treat them with true sincerity.

Accordingly, you will live with a righteous mind, which will, in turn, make your children live righteous lives. Therefore, they will not suffer in life.

A person is incomplete because one lives inside of his mind world, which is false. Living life is difficult because one lives with suffering and burden, and also lives with countless unresolved questions and doubts. The most valuable way of life would be to discard one's mind world, which is false, find the true mind, and be born in the true world and live. The way to become the best parent is to live in a way that will make you become Truth.

V. FINANCE & SUCCESS

JUST AS A COMPUTER NEEDS TO HAVE AI, PEOPLE NEED TO HAVE THE AI-LIKE TRUE WISDOM: A NEW AND COMPLETE LEADERSHIP AND FOLLOWERSHIP

Every person who is born and living in this world has to live with others in society. Depending on their academic performances and also their personalities, there is an immense gap between people as to whether they can succeed or not. In the U.S., statistics show that rather than those who had studied well in school, those who had better personalities eventually became more successful.

"Total person" education is referred to as *Ji-In-Yong* in China, which means wisdom, benevolence, and courage, and it is said that a total person is one who has the qualities of intellect, virtue, and physical strength. However, it is not easy to act with all three: intellect, virtue, and physical strength. To act properly with these virtues, one's mind must become intellect, virtue, and physical strength itself; then, one can naturally do so.

Until now, as people lived in the world, they lived inside their mind worlds, which is made by taking pictures into their memories. Because they only live with what they have experienced, the human mind itself is an illusion, so they cannot know the ways of the world, and they live thinking that only their experiences are right.

From this moment forward, instead of living in the incomplete world, people should live with the complete way of thinking in the complete world. Then they will be righteous, and will live a true life that will last long.

People live inside their own illusory mind worlds, which are illusions. Simply doing false deeds and then dying in the false world is the life of a human. To be without conflicts, hindrances, or blockages, a person should not live in his own mind world, which overlaps the world, and he should discard it so that Truth within him becomes his mind. Then, when one is born again in that land, which is real, they can know all the ways of the world and will not have any unresolved questions or doubts. Also, there is no suffering, burden, or stress. As you have absolutely no delusional thoughts, you can just focus and diligently do your work. You will be wisdom itself, so all that you do is resolved according to nature's flow; and, you can come up with exceptional ideas. You will be a person who has an extra AI-like intelligence. Since you have virtue within the mind, you will know to praise others. Without any harshness in the mind, there will be no conflicts, and you will lead a harmonious life with others. A person who used to have countless delusional thoughts and who would only insist on his own opinion, will now simply focus and diligently do his work. The ultimate way to live a life that cannot possibly get any better is to live a genuine life having become Truth.

There is a saying that people live according to what they have "eaten" in their minds. This is because people live according to what they have in their minds. Those who came to have law within their minds while attending school will make a living practicing law, those who have architecture will make a living by designing buildings, and those who studied computer science and have computers in their minds will make a living with computers. Just like that, one lives with what one has in his mind. Also, even though they are within the same field of law, architecture, or computers, some achieve great success whereas others struggle to barely make a living. This is because people do not have the truthful mind that is able to be devoted to what they do. Those who have many of their own delusional thoughts, which are illusions, cannot devote themselves to what they do because of those delusional thoughts. They keep agonizing over countless thoughts and end up simply wasting their time.

If you only have the mind of Truth in your mind, you can simply do the work that you do and you can become successful. And as your relationships are not self-centered, you will be able to listen to other people, understand them, and treat them with generosity. You will have an accepting mind, which is the mind that can always be generous and understanding.

Now, one who lives with the mind of complete Truth is the best person. In the past, a "total person" was referring to a person with the qualities of intellect, virtue, and physical strength. However, people were not able to become the true, "total person."

Now, a "total person" is one who goes to the Land of Truth, is reborn in the Land of Truth, and lives there. One can live well because he will be truthful and sincere.

In this one and only lifetime:
- There is no one in this world who likes me, and there is no one who acknowledges me either.
- Circumstances and time will not wait for me.
- Always think that now is the best time.
- Behave in a way that will make others like me.
- Make an effort to be second to none in what I do.
- Do not try to achieve from within the false mind.

One can act in this way only when his mind itself becomes the true mind. Even when he is told, "Awaken the sleeping giant inside you," he cannot awaken because he does not have the mind of the world. When one becomes the true mind, the sleeping giant will become awakened on its own, and countless awakening wisdom will follow. Of the different kinds of education, if you receive this character education that is "Human Completion Education" ("Total Person" Education), you can live well since you have become wisdom itself.

This is the true leadership and followership of the new era.

HOW TO SUCCEED

To succeed in any worldly affairs, a person must have the mind that is able to focus wholeheartedly on what he does; only then can one succeed.

A person who has numerous, complicated thoughts in his head will not be able to commit to the work he does, no matter what it is.

It is said that those with good personalities become more successful than people who had good grades in school. This is because a person can only succeed when he can accept what others say rather than having a selfish, self-centered mind. To become successful, one should always be able to accept other people's opinions and devote oneself to what he does without countless cluttered, delusional thoughts. To have a good personality and work hard, you need to have your mind become Truth. Consequently, you can have a great personality and can fully focus on and be diligent with the work that you do, which will lead to success.

THE WAY TO ACHIEVE YOUR GOAL

If a person has a certain goal, he must have the desire in his mind to achieve that goal. When one's mind has nothing else but that goal, and when he takes action, his goal can be quickly achieved.

People fail to achieve their goals because they have countless thoughts. Once people eliminate their minds, which give rise to those thoughts, these minds will disappear. Only when you have no mind at all, can you dedicate yourself to achieving your goal. Then, you can achieve your goal.

CREATIVE THINKING: HOW TO BE CREATIVE

For people to have creativity, they should have the universe mind, which is the living Truth.

To have this, people need to throw away the human mind, which is false, and become the mind of the world, which is true. Then, they will have creativity because they will have wisdom. Creativity does not exist in one's own mind. Creativity only exists in the true mind.

THE POWER OF PERSUASION: HOW TO PERSUADE PEOPLE

To persuade others, you should inspire them to have confidence in you. And your sincere words are what can persuade others. Also, you should make them pay attention to your words. When your mind is solely focused on what you have to say, your words will be persuasive.

HOW TO BECOME RICH

For a person to become rich, one needs to have a heart and mind big enough to have the capacity to be a rich person. One should have confidence in what he does, and have a benevolent mind to be in harmony with other people. In addition, one should not have regrets about the past or worries about the future so that he can just work on what he is doing at that moment.

The way you live today is your life in the future. When you have the mind that is able to devote yourself to today's work with all your might, and when you have a big mind and a personality that can accept others, you can become rich.

When you cleanse your mind so that there are no obstacles and hindrances coming from yourself, your mind becomes the mind that is free from thoughts, which are delusions. And when you work diligently with that mind, focusing only on the work that you do, wisdom emerges and so you can live well.

GETTING A GOOD JOB

Although people look for a good job that suits their interests and personality while providing financial prosperity, it is difficult to find such a suitable job. This is because while jobs in those fields are hard to come by, there are many people who are seeking.

The job you get may not be the job you wanted. However, once you get it, if you dedicate yourself to the work that you do, perform better than others, and have a good personality to get along well with others within the organization, you can succeed.

HOW TO SURVIVE

Since childhood, people living in this world have been fighters in their minds who constantly had to fight invisible battles to be better at school, make more money than others, and do everything better than others. However, those who are big-minded can become successful and achieve what they want in life. Those who are small-minded face obstacles on their way toward their goals because they encounter conflicts in everything they do.

In the U.S., statistics show that rather than those who have good grades in school, those who have better characters and personalities become more successful later in life. When it comes to surviving in this world, one who lives an overly selfish life does not last long. Those who are generous, understanding of others, and big-minded become successful because people around them support and cooperate with them. One can become successful if he changes his mind to the big mind, allowing him to diligently dedicate himself to the work that he does with that big mind. The way to change one's mind to a big mind is to eliminate one's conceptions and customs.

HOW TO SAVE MONEY: KEY MINDSET

If you want to save money, eliminate the mind that wants to spend money to compensate for your inferiority. Also, only spend money when necessary.

Be conscious of your current financial situation: do not spend money if you do not have money. When you work hard, you will not have enough time to spend money, so you will end up not spending it. People spend money due to their sense of inferiority, which is their false mind. Once you discard this false mind, you will not waste as much money.

HOW TO FIND YOUR TRUE TALENT AND TO BE SUCCESSFUL

Everyone is born with different talents. However, when two people are doing the same thing in life, the one who always works hard and is consistent is unbeatable. We can often see that a person who silently perseveres becomes successful despite the lack of talent. When one eliminates his mind and has the biggest mind, which is the mind of oneness, he can focus solely on the task in front of him. Anyone who does that can become successful. Therefore, the truly talented person is the one who cleanses his mind rather than a person who has innate talent.

HOW TO ORGANIZE OR SYSTEMATIZE YOUR LIFE

When people try to organize or systematize their lives, it is not easy to do so from their minds, which are their thoughts. This is because people live with the minds they have within themselves. When one eliminates the framework of his mind, his life will naturally be organized and systematized.

One's mind is the karma, habits, and body, and are one's fixed conceptions and customs. When these do not exist, one's mind becomes Truth, which is the Origin, and will automatically be organized and systematized. It is not easy to organize or systematize one's life within his false fixed conceptions and customs because these are falseness. When there is no falseness and one becomes Truth, he has a big mind that can accept all things in the world.

People are used to looking at their lives through their own fixed conceptions, habits and customs, so they would not know the answer to how to organize and systematize their lives. But when they become Truth, they will realize how to do so on their own.

HOW TO BE A FAST LEARNER

We live our lives trying to learn something—at school and even after we start working. Just as someone who crams cannot do well at school, a person who studies consistently before and after the class will do well. People cannot focus on their studies or do well because of their countless thoughts.

People have thoughts, which are the agonies in their minds. So, once they discard that mind, those thoughts will disappear, and they can just focus on what they do and dedicate themselves to it. As a result, they will be good at whatever it is that they undertake.

The way to become successful in life is to simply concentrate and diligently focus on what you do without thoughts—such a person is attractive. The way to be a fast learner is also to have a mind that is focused on taking interest and trying to learn.

HOW TO LIVE A GOOD LIFE

There is only one world, but the number of different worries people have is as many as the number of people living in the world, and people are living with suffering, burden, and stress.

People are self-centered and they live in their mind worlds with as much stress as the minds they have accumulated. So, the wisest way of life would be for people to have the mind of the world that embraces the world. They can then adapt themselves to the world, always be positive, and can live stress-free, happy lives.

Only when you break free from the narrow and false human mind, become the mind of the world, and live in the world, can you then live without hindrances and obstacles. Once you do the meditation to eliminate your false body and mind, you can become successful in life.

HOW TO CHANGE YOUR LIFE FOR THE BETTER: LIFE ADVICE

The reason and purpose why humans are born into this world is to become complete, eternally never die, and live happily. If you are to live a life of happiness and freedom without suffering and burden, you should first discard your incomplete, false self. By doing so, if you recover the complete self before anything else, you will always live a joyful, happy life.

A person's first priority is to discard the incomplete self, which only gives suffering, burden, and stress, and find one's true self, be born in the true world, and live. Then, you will be successful in life and in whatever you do.

Above all, become a true person. Then you can live well without feeling stressed about what you do. Now is the era to eliminate the self, the stress.

VI. SPIRITUALITY & BELIEF

HOW TO REACH ENLIGHTENMENT

People commonly say that they have enlightened, but there is no one in this world who truly did. If someone had truly enlightened, this person should be able to make others also enlighten—otherwise, this person would not be an enlightened person.

People's consciousness should not be living inside their own illusionary minds, which are the accumulation of their lives lived.

After discarding one's illusionary mind, one will enlighten as much as one changes from the self-centered mind to the great universe mind that is Truth.

Complete enlightenment is having God within one's mind. One who is born in Heaven is a completely enlightened person.

One who has achieved human completion is a person who has enlightened all. When the human mind changes to the universe mind, which is God, one will have many, many enlightenments.

TRUTH

We have learned that Truth is something that is eternal and unchanging. The definition of Truth is the non-material existence that is eternal, unchanging, and alive. In this world, no one was able to teach Truth because people do not have Truth.

Countless people have come and gone in this world. However, none of them were able to teach Truth because there was no one who was Truth. Only when Truth comes in human form can that existence teach Truth. It is only when the people who are Truth come to this world that the true world will be created by these people.

Electricity became available to utilize because Edison founded electricity and brought it to the world. In the same way, it is only when Truth comes that it will be possible for this existence to show people Truth, and make people go to, be born into, and live in the Land of Truth.

This is how the material world is born in the world of Truth, which is the world of *Jung* (Spirit) and *Shin* (Soul), and lives eternally without death.

This is the era of human completion and it is the era to become enlightened beings and saints. This is achieved when the existence of Truth comes as people.

WHAT ARE THE SPIRIT AND SOUL?

People commonly think that one lives on after he dies because his Spirit and Soul exist. However, there is no Spirit and Soul in people.

All material things in this world exist and act while that material entity is still alive. When it does not exist, it does not exist.

Let us suppose that there is a dead person here. This person cannot think or cry out in pain even if a part of the body is cut out or pierced with a knife. It would simply be a piece of material where there is nothing, and once this material is burned and eliminated, there is nothing. For all material things that are born in this world, once they disappear after existing in a certain shape and form, there is nothing that remains.

If the Spirit and Soul are to exist, the self has to disappear. Then, the mind has to go to the Origin and be born again from there—only then do the Spirit and Soul exist. To be reborn from there means the masters of Truth create that Spirit and Soul. Only then do the true Spirit and Soul exist.

Those who have the Spirit and Soul of Truth within can live eternally without life or death. Only the one whose false self has completely died while living, and is reborn as Truth, has the Spirit and Soul.

HEAVEN (THE REAL HEAVEN)

No one who lives in this world has even seen God; no one has seen or gone to Heaven. The Heaven that people say they have seen are all illusions, not the real one.

All the religious scriptures say that "God and Heaven are within your mind." However, because humans are sinners and incomplete, they do not have Heaven, which is God's world. This is because people live inside their own minds. Since their minds are not the mind of the world, neither God nor Heaven exists within them.

If one repents one's sins by discarding the life lived and the self, completely gets rid of one's mind world, which is a false world, and goes to the true world, then God exists within oneself. Heaven exists within oneself.

People think that they go to Heaven when this physical body dies. However, while living, when people's minds become the true world's mind, and they are reborn there, then this land, this place, which is Heaven, is in their minds at all times. As such, one is born and living in Heaven without life or death.

People are unable to see neither God nor Heaven because the world of Truth does not exist in their minds. One who has gotten rid of one's karma, habits, and body is born and lives in Heaven at all times.

THE METHOD TO SEE AND KNOW GOD

People cannot see God because God does not exist inside their minds.

God, which created all creations in this universe, is the non-material, living existence that is alive and exists. However, this existence cannot be seen with the human eyes. This existence is the infinite universe emptiness. It exists as the Spirit and Soul, which is the body and mind of the universe. This existence created all of creation.

All material forms live according to their lifespans and then disappear. But when the body and mind of the universe, the Spirit and Soul, come as human beings, it is the *Jung* (Spirit) and *Shin* (Soul). When this existence creates again and people are reborn as *Jung* and *Shin*, they become Truth. They become eternally living immortals. Thereafter, because people have Heaven within their minds, they live forever. The world that is born again as Truth does not disappear.

To see and know God, people must eliminate their bodies and minds, which are their sins. Subsequently, the great universe itself, which is Truth, exists within people's minds, and one can see and know God because it exists within one's mind. When this existence comes as human beings, this existence will carry out the creation of the Holy Spirit and Holy Soul. This existence is that of the saviors who make people be born in Heaven and live there.

WHAT IS THE MEANING OF LIFE?

Everyone is born into this world, lives, and then just dies. Death means to disappear. This is what death is. The reason and purpose of being born into the world and living is to achieve human completion and live eternally. If one does not live eternally, then one's life has no meaning. When one becomes complete and lives forever, works in the true world, and lives, one's life has meaning.

WHAT HAPPENS WHEN YOU DIE AND HOW NOT TO DIE?

All things in this world come from the emptiness that is nothingness and return to this emptiness. In other words, a material existence comes from the place of nothingness, subsists, and then returns to that place of nothingness. Humans also come from this place of nothingness and return to that place of nothingness.

Let's assume that there is a dead person here. This person cannot think, and cannot cry out in pain even if pierced with a knife. When a person dies, one cannot think or act as they did when living. Once that person has been cremated, nothing remains. This is why there is nothing when a person dies. Just as a car cannot function without its battery, dying means to disappear completely. This is what death is.

To be born again, or to be reborn, refers to going back to the place of nothingness and being born anew as Truth in the true world. This world is Heaven and Paradise. Unless one has been born in this world while living, that person just disappears upon death since there is no Heaven and Paradise within that person's mind.

When the masters of the world who are Truth come to this world, and one's mind becomes one with the mind of the owner, which is the Original Foundation of the universe, the self of the past completely disappears.

At this time, when the owners create the true world, which is the new world, through the words, one can be born again, reborn. When born anew as the body and mind of Truth, one can live eternally in this land, right here.

CLEAR MIND: HOW TO CLEANSE YOUR MIND WITH MEDITATION

The reason and purpose for cleansing the mind is that the human mind is an illusion and false. If one gets rid of the illusionary, false mind, is born into the world, and lives, one's life in this world will be that of boundless comfort and freedom. One is born into this eternally living, immortal world and lives without death—how fortunate is this?

Until now, there has not been a way to cleanse the mind, but now there is a method to eliminate the mind. When there is no mind, you will have wisdom, and you will always be happy.

The human mind consists of the karma, habits, and body. When one discards the karma, habits, and body within, only Truth remains. And when one is reborn in the Land of Truth, one achieves human completion and eternally never dies. This is the era of human completion. To cleanse the mind means to eliminate the false mind—this is what it means to cleanse. When you do meditation to eliminate the false mind, you can achieve completion.

HOW TO FIND YOUR TRUE SELF

The true self is the self that has been born as Truth. Because people live inside their sins and karma, they do not have their true selves. There is no one in this world who has been born as the true self. The one who is born as the body and mind of God is the one who is born as the true self.

When the self who is the sinner completely disappears, becomes the Spirit and Soul of the true world, and is born again, that person is the one who has found the true self. One who has accomplished his true self has God, which is Truth, in his mind, and has Heaven. For this, one has to be born again through the words of the world's masters. Then, one will find his true self.

PEACE OF MIND

There is no peace in the human mind because people follow their greed and live in accordance with this greed. The human mind takes pictures of what belongs to the world. Filled with these stolen pictures, the human mind is the mind of sin, agony, burden, and stress. When you erase the illusionary human mind, along with the false life lived, habits, and body, then the true mind exists. When you are born again, you have the universe mind, which is Truth. This mind is the mind of inner peace.

ACTS OF KINDNESS

While we are living, we consider it to be an act of kindness to help others when they are in trouble, whether by providing them with material goods or in other ways.

However, Jesus said that there is no righteous person in this world. Just because people help others in this way does not mean that they are good people. Since people live inside their false minds, the entire concept of good or bad is not of the true mind.

Jesus said that there is no righteous person in this world because there is no Truth in the illusionary world, which is one's own mind. Real Truth is when one's mind becomes the universe mind, which is Truth. Then, the deed done would be Truth. When you discard the human mind, you become the universe mind. When you act from this universe mind, you will not have any mind that you have done something. This is the mind of freedom, and it is truly good because it does not discern between good and evil.

It is a true act of kindness to become a true person by eliminating the human mind and performing deeds in the true world. Only one who is born in this eternally living, immortal land will be able to act with true kindness. This is one's blessings.

HOW TO BRING RELIGIONS TOGETHER

There are many religions in this world, and even within a single religion, there are numerous different denominations. Each denomination and religion claim that they are right and the others are all heresy and cults. Then, how do we know which place is the real one?

Where you can become true would be the real place of Truth.

Humans are incomplete because their mind worlds are the minds that were created by taking pictures of the things of the world, which is real. Therefore, these mind worlds are false.

People are incomplete and false because they do not live in the Land of Truth, which is the world, but live inside their mind worlds that are false. Because people interpret the religious scriptures from within the false mind worlds based on their false conceptions, they could not interpret correctly and ended up creating countless denominations.

The way for this world to become one and to bring religions together is for people to discard their human minds, which are false, be born in the true mind, which is real, and have the world of Truth within their minds. All religions can then come together, and we can live in a world where all are one without boundaries created by philosophies, ideologies, academics, or countries.

Starting from the twenty-first century, everyone can live in the world where there is no conflict if all people become Truth and are born into and live in the true world, which never dies.

THE MOST IMPORTANT THING IN THE WORLD

The basic human necessities are food, clothes, and a house to sleep in. However, even when all of these needs are met, people are still not happy and always yearn for more. The more they have, the more they want. The innumerable desires and thoughts in people's brains do not cease to exist, resulting in a life of agony and burden.

Because people are illusory and are living in the false world, they have no true wisdom and do not know the ways of the world or Truth. The reason and purpose humans are born into this world is not just to live for seventy-eighty years and then die and disappear; they have come to this world to live.

The reason and purpose people are born into this world is to go from the illusory world to the true world. The most important thing in the world is to be born in the true world and live amassing your own blessings in that world. This is a truly happy life.

THE REASON WHY PEOPLE CANNOT SEE THE CREATORS THAT ARE TRUTH

Since the creators that are Truth do not exist within the human mind, people can neither see nor know Truth. People believe that Truth exists in some kind of vague state. For people to be able to see and know Truth, the existence of Truth must come to this world as human beings and teach Truth; then, they can see and know Truth.

WHAT IS RESURRECTION?

Being born again or being born anew is resurrection. For people to be born again or to be born anew, there must be no life lived, habits, and body of the false self, which is incomplete. Resurrection is being born again as the body and mind of the universe, which is Truth.

When none of the false self exists, and one goes to the Origin of the universe, which is Truth, the Origin becomes one's mind. Then, when one is born again from there, no false self exists, so one can be born again as the true self. The masters of the world, who are the existence of Truth, can give birth.

No one has seen God, which is Truth, and no one has gone to Heaven. This is because the true world does not exist within one's mind; therefore, one cannot go there.

Resurrection is when one's mind becomes Truth and one is born in the Land of Truth; this is resurrection and the eternally living Heaven.

WHAT IS THE RAPTURE?

There was an occasion when the Dami Mission Church made a great commotion throughout the world about the rapture.

Declarations saying only those being raptured, those getting marked with the seal, or only a selected 144,000 people will go to Heaven are false declarations if they are not actually being realized right now. None of the prophecies with a fixed date have ever been correct, and prophecies saying that when there are 144,000 people, they would be saved and become complete are false if they are not actually taking place.

No one can be born as Truth without eliminating their sins and karma and being reborn as Truth. There must be a method that enables the falseness to become Truth. For anyone to be reborn in Truth, which is the land of completion, it is only possible if they know and have faith in the will of Truth; only then will they be able to achieve it.

Those who try to achieve Truth without repenting will not be able to achieve it.

The rapture means to ascend into Heaven.

When you discard the false world in your mind, which is the world of pictures, the true world, which is Heaven, becomes your mind. When you are born from there, you are born in Heaven, which means that you have been raptured.

People living in the false world are raptured when the existence that are the masters of Truth give them birth in Heaven, which is Truth.

The rapture is being reborn and resurrected in the true world. To be raptured means to go from the false world to the true world.

WHY DO WE LIVE?

The reason humans are born into this world and live is to live eternally. The reason and purpose of human life is to live. Humans are incomplete. People live in their false mind worlds and end up disappearing.

In the age of incompletion, people live inside their own illusionary mind worlds instead of living in the world, which is Truth, because their minds overlap the world. And since they live in illusionary mind worlds, they are a nonexistent illusion and end up dying.

When there is no false world or self, one will go to the universe, which is Truth. And when one is reborn from there, he can be born in the true world and live without death.

People need to be born into the world and live; they need to be born into the true world and live without death. Nothing else in the world should be more important than this.

People often question whether we live our lives to eat or to live, and the answer is, "To live." This is the singular most important thing in the world and the purpose of life.

CHANGE YOUR LIFE

While living in this world, people carry stress, suffering, and burden because matters do not work out according to their minds of greed, resulting in unsatisfied desires. This is generally how people live. Therefore, one has to change one's life to a stress-free life.

To change your life, you should get rid of the mind, the stress, have the true mind, and be born in the true world and live there. Consequently, you will have no stress and will live well according to nature's flow because you will always have wisdom in life. Then, your life will change completely.

HOW TO SEE AND KNOW GOD

I once heard a member of the clergy say, "Although there are countless people who believe in God in this world, there are none who have seen God."

People can only know, speak, and live according to what they have in their minds.

The existence of God is the emptiness, which is the entire universe. It exists as the Spirit and Soul of the non-material existence, which is the existence of Truth. This existence has created all material forms, and every manifestation in the world is this existence. When the Spirit and Soul of Truth, which are this existence, come as human beings, this land, right here, which is the world of Truth, is created in people's minds, and this is the Land of Truth that is Heaven.

The reason why people cannot see God is that they do not have God in their minds. The human mind is the karma, habits, and body, and these are false. Your mind becomes the universe emptiness itself, which is Truth, when all of these karma, habits, and body are eliminated. Then, you can see God because God exists within your mind. Your mind is the universe itself when you disappear completely. This is the way to see and know God and also the creators that come as human beings. God is the Way, the Truth, and the Life. No one can be born into Heaven without going through God. One can only see and know God from the true mind.

HOW TO UNDERSTAND THE BIBLE WELL

The Bible is a prophecy book about the time of completion that will come someday when humans can become complete and live eternally in Heaven. The words in the Bible are spoken from the perspective of Truth, so it is very difficult for people who are living in false worlds to understand those words. For example, in the Bible, it says that Jesus was resurrected three days after his death and walked out of his tomb. This means that by dying from inside his own mind, which is like a stone tomb, he escaped the mind world and was born in the land of Truth, which is the true world.

In order to understand the Bible, one should discard one's self and the false world from the false world and be born in the true world—then the Bible can be understood. The Bible is spoken from Truth, so one can understand it all when he eliminates his mind world, which is false, and goes to the world of Truth, which is real. One can also live eternally in the Land of Truth while living. The way to understand the Bible is to discard the false world and be reborn in the true world.

HOW TO SEE HEAVEN AND GO THERE

Heaven is the Kingdom of God that is Truth. Truth exists within your mind. The way to see and know God that is Truth is when one's karma, habits, and body do not exist and when the universe emptiness itself exists in one's mind. When one is reborn from that emptiness, this place is Heaven.

When your self, who is false, and your false mind world disappear, you go to the universe emptiness that is Truth. From there, the owners of the universe will resurrect this world as the world of Truth.

All material forms in this world can only last as long as their life spans. However, the world that is created inside people's minds is the world of Truth, and all material forms are also Truth. So there is no death.

This is the creation of the Holy Spirit and Holy Soul. Heaven and earth are created as the Holy Spirit and Holy Soul inside people's minds and, thereafter, will last for eternity.

Creation of the Holy Spirit and Holy Soul can only be done by people who are the masters of the world. Each person is the master, and all exist inside one's mind. Therefore, it is the era when the purpose of human existence, human dignity, and human rights are fulfilled. The person is the master, will go to Heaven and Paradise, and will live without death.

You will not die, only if you are born into and live in Heaven while you are still alive.

For humans, although it seems that they are living in the real world, they do not live there because they are living inside the mind world that overlaps the world.

Because people live in the illusionary world, their minds are not righteous, and they cannot see the world for what it is.

However, when you enlighten to and live in the real world, you can know the principles of the world and can become a *complete* person.

This book, which has been written from the perspective of Truth, explains the ways of this world. It is the alternative solution to help you find what you are looking for and achieve everything.

Did you know

that everything you have been searching for is within your mind? Truth, Heaven, happiness, success and health are all within your mind.

The top 10 things that people are looking for. What are you looking for?

1. Go to a world where one will not die and live eternally
2. Be happy
3. Be successful
4. Have the ability to accomplish one's goals
5. Be healthy
6. Have peace within
7. Become free from useless thoughts and truly focus on the present
8. Break bad habits
9. Always have a grateful mind
10. Have successful relationships

If you would like to learn how to achieve what you are looking for, email:

books@thelifeanswers.com